Thomas Pope Blount

Sir Tho. Pope Blount's Essays on Several Subjects

Thomas Pope Blount

Sir Tho. Pope Blount's Essays on Several Subjects

ISBN/EAN: 9783337092191

Printed in Europe, USA, Canada, Australia, Japan

Cover: Foto ©Thomas Meinert / pixelio.de

More available books at **www.hansebooks.com**

Sir *Tho. Pope Blount*'s

ESSAYS

ON SEVERAL

SUBJECTS.

Conamur Tenues Grandia.
Hor. Lib. 1. Od. 6.

The Third Impreſſion; *with very*
Large Additions.
Beſides a New ESSAY *of* Religi-
on.
And an Alphabetical INDEX *to*
the Whole.

L O N D O N,
Printed for *Richard Bently,* in
Ruſſel-Street in *Covent-Gar-*
den: MDCXCVII.

Reader,

I *Here present you with the* Third Impref-fion *of my* ESSAYS; *to which there is now ad-ded above a* Third Part. *I shall only tell you,* That *they are intended purely for your Service, and there-fore if they can afford you either* Inftruction *or* Di-verfion, *I am Satisfied.*

A N

Alphabetical INDEX.

A.

B.

C.

A 3 Customes;

An Alphabetical INDEX.

Hu-

An Alphabetical INDEX.

An Alphabetical INDEX.

ESSAY

ESSAY I.

That INTEREST *governs the* WORLD: *And that* Popery *is nothing but* Prieſt-Craft, *or an Invention of the* Prieſt's *to get* Money.

INTEREST is that *Univerſal Monarch*, to which all other Empires are Tributaries. It is the great *Idol* to which the World bows: To *this* we pay our devouteſt Homage, and give it not only our *Knees* but our *Hearts.*

Intereſt is of that *Magnetick* Quality, that our Affections are almoſt irreſiſtably attracted by it: It is the *Pole* to which we turn, and we commonly frame our Judgments ac-

cording

cording to its direction. Men generally look more after the *Dowry*, than the *Beauty* of Truth, its correspondency to their *Interest*, than its evidence to their Underſtandings: And therefore whenever *Truth* and *Intereſt* are put into the balance, *Intereſt* ſtill turns the *Scale*; moſt Men judging of *Truth*, juſt as *Brutus* did of Virtue, that it is but *Nomen inane*, a meer empty ſound; And that no wife Man would ever ſuffer himſelf to be canted out of his Profit and Advantage. An uſeful Error (then) hath often found free Admiſſion, when important Truths, but contrary to Mens Preconceptions or *Intereſts*, have been forbidden entrance. Temporal Expectations bring in whole Droves to the *Mahumetan* Faith; and we too well know the ſame holds Thouſands in the *Romiſh*. An advantagious Cauſe never wanted Proſelytes. The Eagles will be where the Carcaſe is: And that ſhall have the Faith of moſt which is beſt able to pay 'em for't.

In

In all Ages of the World, *Interest* govern'd Mankind, and therefore we see the wifeft Law-makers ftill built upon this Foundation; making it the *Intereft* of the Community to put their Laws in Execution; hence *Plutarch* reported *Solon* to have faid, That he had fo fram'd his Laws, that the Citizens were fenfible, it was more their *Intereft* to oblerve them, than to violate them. Almighty God, when he firft gave Laws to his own People the *Jews*, was pleas'd to confider them as a worldly covetous fort of People; and therefore to make their Obedience the more eafie, he gives 'em a Conftitution agreeable to their Genius, promifing 'em all forts of Temporal Bleffings, fuch as *Poffef-fion of the Land, Freedom from Bondage*, &c. He very well knew, that *worldly Intereft* would go a great deal further, than the pure, Intrinfick worth of Vertue and Goodnefs; and therefore that the fureft-way to enforce his Laws, was

by

by ſtriking upon their Affections. Thus is God fain to deal with Man, juſt as the *Husbandman* in the *Goſpel* did; by proffering his *Penny* before he can prevail with 'em to work in his *Vineyard*. Chriſt obſerv'd, That the Multitudes throng'd after him more for the *Loaves* and *Fiſhes*, than for his Doctrine; intimating that few lov'd him *Gratis*, but to make advantage by him : And this the *Devil* knew too well, when he charg'd *Job* with it, ſaying, *Does* Job *ſerve God for nought ?* In a word, *Gain* and *Advantage* is that which every Man aims at; be the Buſineſs never ſo *Bad*, you may have it done for Money; and be it never ſo *Good*, you cannot have it done without. Let us but caſt our Eyes upon thoſe two Religions, the *old Heatheniſh* and the *Romiſh*, and we ſhall ſoon ſee their reſpective *Prieſts* offering Incenſe to the *Unrighteous Mammon*. Whoever looks into the whole Body (or rather *Chaos*) of the Religion of the *Ancient Hea-*

Heathens, will find, that it was chiefly made up of fuch ftrange and extravagant Stories of their *Gods* and *Heroes,* that it became loathfome to the moft Intelligent Part of themfelves. Their very *Myfteria Sacra* were fo full of all wickednefs and filthy Abominations, that it was counted the very wifeft Point in all their Religion, to take fuch mighty care as they did, for the keeping them Secret. Such confufed Notions had they of their *Elyfium,* that the Epithet of *Shades* belong'd more properly to the *Darknefs,* than the *Refrefhment* ; and was a Reward fit for the *Votaries* of thofe ambiguous *Oracles* they confulted ! In fhort, their Religion was all wrapt up in Clouds, and Darknefs : Many of their *Worfhips* were nothing but a Solemnity of the Fouleft Vices ; and their *Divinity* taught 'em only to vitiate *Morality.* In *Rome,* their Religion was grown to that height of abfurdity, that one tells us in *Cicero,* That even

B 3 the

the *Roman* Priests themselves did to such a degree contemn their own Devotions and Ceremonies, that they could scarce forbear smiling when they met in the Street, to think how cleaverly the Cheat went on. In a Word, never any one scorn'd any thing more, than *Cæsar* himself did his own *Gods*, and, as *Tertullian* observes, would often please himself, in that he was able to make his *Gods* feel the Power of his Anger.

But to be a little more Particular; No sooner was that which was called by the name of Religion, planted among the *Heathen*, but immediately their *Priests*, a pert forward sort of Men, stood up, and insinuated to the People the absolute Necessity of *Sacrifices* ; and that these *Sacrifices* cou'd never be acceptable to the *Gods*, unless they were offer'd up by uncorrupt, Sanctified Hands, meaning *their own*. How beneficial these *Sacrifices* were to the *Heathen Priests*, you may easily imagine ;

gine; fince according to the old
Proverb, 'tis an ill Cook that can't
lick his own Fingers. And unlefs
their *Priefts* had found advantage
by it, certainly they would never
have enjoin'd the People fuch an un-
accountable way of Worfhip. For
what a ftrange and uncouth Belief
was it to think that the moft proper way to attone and pacifie their
Offended Gods, was by flaying and
facrificing *Innocent Creatures ?* But
as unreafonable as this may feem to
Men of Honefty and Sincerity, yet
the *Heathen Priefts* (men wholly
actuated by Intereft) conceiv'd different fentiments. For whatever
contributed to their advantage, they
never boggled at; and the *Profpe-
rum Scelus* was all the *Vertue* they
defir'd. Hence then it was, that the
Heathens turn'd Religion into a
Trade, wherein the moft gainful
was their *Sacrifices : Mendicantes vi-
catim Deos ducunt* ; a God was then
as fit an Object for Charity, as now
a broken Arm, or a Wooden Leg :

Nor did they confider their Gods any otherwife, than for their own Intereft. Thus then thefe fubtile, crafty *Heathen Priefts*, obferving that mankind was for the moft part ill-natur'd and not apt to oblige others without fome reward, as alfo judging of God Almighty by themfelves, did at firft conceive the *Gods* to be like their *Eaftern* Princes, before whom no Man might come empty-handed: Hence, I fay, the crafty Sacerdotal Order (who were maintain'd and grew rich out of the Follies and Paffions of Men) did above all things inculcate and propagate this Opinion: And for as much as good part of the Offerings fell to the *Prieft's* fhare: Therefore they foon left off *Pythagoras's* poor Inftitution of *Frankincenfe*, *Fruits*, *Flowers*, &c. Which lafted till their *Gods* (or to fpeak truly their *Priefts*) grew fo covetous, that nothing but the Bloud of *Beafts* could fatiate them, and fo fell to *Sacrificing* firft *Beafts*, then *Men*, *Women* and *Children*,

dren, and the very *Gods* themfelves, if they could have got them, and (as a late Author obferves) all this was to bring Roft-meat to the Priefts.

Was it not alfo from the fame root, I mean, the covetous Temper of the *Heathen Priefts*, from whence fprung up the firft *Idolatry* that ever was in the World? I know very well, that many of the *Ancients* haveexcus'dtheHeathen's*Polytheifm*, by telling us, That they worfhip'd not divers Gods, but one and the fame, under feveral Appellations, and Names, according to thofe various Benefits they had received from him, or thofe divers Apprehenfions they had of him. As *Lipfius*, fpeaking of the *Gods* of the *Stoicks*, fays, They were rather *Multitudo Nominum, quàm Numinum*, a Multitude of Names, rather than of Natures. And St. *Auftin*, in his *De Civitate Dei cap.* 24. brings in the *Heathens*, pleading for themfelves, That they were not fo ridiculoufly ignorant,

as

as to think *Vertue*, or *Fortune*, or
the Reft,, *Gods*, but only divers Expreffions of the fame *Deity*. Take
it (then) with this charitable Inter-
pretation, ftill thefe *Godlins*, or *Un-
der-Gods*, were of mighty advantage
to the *Priefts*, and brought in abun-
dance of Grift to their Mill. For
thofe *Spiritual Sharpers* knew well
enough, That the celebrating many
Gods, and the introducing feveral
Worfhips of them, would turn
much more to their Profit and Advantage, than the fingle Worfhip
of the *Supreme God*: And therefore
rather than want *Gods*, they took
care to coin a Sufficient number of
them ; there being no lefs (according to *Varro*) than thirty thoufand
Heathen Deities. And that the
Priefts (let 'em pretend to what
they would) confulted not herein
the Good of the People, fo much,
as their own particular *Interefts*,does
moft manifeftly appear,by the choice
they made of their *Gods* ; moft of
whom (we know) were renowned
for

for nothing fo much as for their Vices: *Mars*, a Bloudy **God** ; *Bacchus*, a Drunken **God** ; *Mercury*, a Cheating **God** ; and fo proportionably in the feveral kinds all the reft ; **Nay**, even their great Capital **God**, *Jupiter*, was guilty of almoft all the Capital Vices. And therefore no Wonder, we find fuch grofs and extravagant things in the old *Heathenifh* Religion, when the very *Gods*, whom they Worfhipp'd, gave fuch encouragement thereunto by their own lewd example : And where the *Gods* are naught, who can expect the *Religion* fhould be good; for 'tis the Nature of all Religions, to encline Men to imitate him whom they Worfhip.

Another Artifice whereby the *Heathen Priefts* us'd to make themfelves valu'd and efteem'd, was that Invention of theirs, the fetting up of *Oracles*. 'Tis hard to fay, who were guilty of the greater folly, the *ignorant Heathen*, who believ'd thofe Prædictions to come from *Heaven* ;

or

or those *Superstitious Christians*, who thought they came from the *Devil* ; since they were both under a grofs Miftake. For certainly to any Man, who is unbiafs'd in Opinion, and who dares fuffer himfelf to think beyond, the narrow Rules of his Education, they cannot appear to be any thing but the meer juggling and Impofture of the *Heathen Priefts*. But fince a learned Divine of the Church of *England* (Mr. *John Edwards*, in his farther *Enquiry* into fome Remarkable *Texts* of *Scripture*) has thought fit to fall foul upon this Opinion of Mine : He affirming, that the *Oracles* were firft invented by the *Devil*, and that the *Priefts* in this Matter acted only *Minifterially* ; I hope, I fhall not tire the Patience of the *Reader*, if in my own Defence I enlarge upon this Subject, and even from the very beft Authorities prove this my Affertion. *Theodoret* fays, That *Theophilus*, Bifhop of *Alexandria*, fhew'd the Inhabitants of that Town, the

Hollow

Hollow Statues, into which the *Priests* privately crept to deliver their *Oracles*. When the Temple of *Æsculapius*, in *Cilicia*, was by *Constantine's* Order pull'd down *Eusebius* in the Life of this *Emperour* tells us, they chafed thence, not a *God*, nor a *Dæmon*, but the *Cheat*, that had so long deluded the People. *He adds*, that in general, in the demolish'd *Idols*, they found no *Gods* at all nor *Dæmons*, nor so much as a melancholy Shade, or obscure Sight; but only some *Hay*, *Straw*, or *Ordure*, or the Bones of dead Men. The same *Eusebius*, in the fourth Book of his *Evangelical Preparation*, says, That in his time, the most famous Prophets amongst the *Pagans*, and their most celebrated *Divines*, of whom some were *Magistrates* of their Cities, were compell'd by torments to discover the very Particulars of all the Cheats of the *Oracles*. *Osbourn* in his Advice to his Son, is of the Opinion, That the *Oracles* of Old were nothing but the Impostures of
Priests

Priests, who poſſibly might have the knack of ſpeaking either in the *Throat* or *Belly,* (as our *Ventriloquiſts* now a days can,) which ſeem'd to be a Voice at a great Diſtance. But *others* fancy, That it is not improbable, but that ſort of *Trumpet,* which multiplies the ſound, might not then be altogether unknown : And that perhaps, Sir *Samuel Moreland* has but reviv'd this Secret, which formerly the *Pagan Prieſts* were Maſters of ; tho' they choſe rather to get profit by concealing it than honour by publiſhing it. And that which induces many to believe this laſt Opinion, is from the aſſurance that *Athanaſius Kircher* gives us, That *Alexander* had one of theſe Inſtruments, by which he made himſelf be heard by his whole Army at the ſame time. There were no Countries obſerv'd to be ſo full of *O-racles,* as thoſe that were moſt Mountainous and by conſequence full of Holes and Caverns ; ſuch as *Bœotia,* which as *Plutarch* tells us, was anciently

ciently thronged with 'em. ' But at
the fame time 'tis worth noting,
That the *Bæotians* were counted the
fillieft and moft ignorant People in
the World ; And therefore it was
the moft proper Country that could
be for *Oracles,* being full of *Blockheads* and *Caverns.* Now, the pretence of *Divine Exhalations* was one
main thing that render'd thefe *Caverns* fo very neceffary : For according to *Plutarch's* vain Philofophy, we are to fuppofe, that the Predictions of the *Oracles* were perform'd by *Exhalation* or vapour
drawn from the Earth ; and this is
the very reafon he gives of their
Being, that they were for a time nou-
rifh'd by thofe *Exhalations* ; and
when *thofe* ceafed and were exhau-
fted, the *Oracles* famifh'd and dy'd,
for want of their accuftom'd Sufte-
nance. But how fo great a Man as
Plutarch feems to be in other things,
could entertain fuch a trifling Opinion, 'tis not eafie to imagine.

Again, *Caverns* of themfelves are
. apt

apt to affect one with a certain Horror, which does not a little advance Superstition ; and in things that are only to make Impressions on the Imaginations of Men, nothing ought to be neglected. Besides, these *Cavities* made the Voice sound much bigger, and caus'd rebounding *Ecchoes*, which imprinted a sort of awful Terror in all that approach'd it. Hence the *Poets* tell us, That the *Pythian Priestesses* strain'd their Voices, so much beyond the pitch of Nature, that they appear'd to be more than *Humane.* I cannot but wonder to see, how very zealous Mr. *Edwards* in his Discourse of the *Oracles* seems to be in asserting the Truth of their *Predictions*, when it is most notorious, that no *Almanack-Maker* writes with less certainty of the Weather, than *they* generally pronounced about future Events ; and if their *Answers* were not directly false, yet they were so Ambiguous, or at least so Obscure, that many times there needed another

ther

ther *Oracle* to explain 'em. As to
the common obfervation concerning
the *Decay* of *Oracles* at the coming
of our Bleffed *Saviour*, 'tis but a
meer fancy; for my part, I do not
in the leaft value any *Oracle* or Sentence, that may be brought to that
purpofe being well affur'd, that they
were but the meer Forgeries of
Primitive Chriftians, whofe blind
intemperate Zeal did tempt 'em to
forge not only *Sentences* but *whole
Authors*, as any who have not read
Hiftories themfelves, may find in
Cafaubon's Exercitations on *Baronius*,
Blondel on the *Sybils*, as alfo the
Decree of Pope *Gelafias*, who amongft
other Counterfeit Authors does pro-
hibit Counterfeit Prophets, Counterfeit Gofpels, and Counterfeit Acts
of the Apoftles. Befides, I would
fain know what fome Men mean
by the *ceafing* of *Oracles* at the coming of *Chrift*: If they mean, that
Oracles were then quite filent, that's
utterly falfe.' For *Plutarch* tells us,
that in his time, which was after
C   *Chrift,*

Christ, the *Oracle* at *Delphos* in *Phocis,* as also that at *Lebadia,* a Town in *Bæotia,* did still give Answers. Again, if they mean only, that *Oracles* were much out of Request at the coming of *Christ* ; I answer, so they were long before his coming, witness a very good Author, *Marcus Tullius Cicero,* who died some Years before *Christ* was born. Yet it appears by his second Book of *Divination,* that *Oracles* were so much gon to decay long before his time, that in his days there was nothing more Contemptible. Now in short, that which did so much contribute to the keeping up the great Credit and Reputation of these *Oracles,* for so many Ages, was the mighty favour and deference shew'd 'em by the greatest Princes : And therefore we find that however ignorant the People were of these Matters, yet all things lay open to the view of the Prince, who made use of this set of Men upon a Politick Design ; for *they* upon all Occasions were

ready

ready to promote the *Interest* and
Ambitious Defigns of the prefent
Rulers. And therefore, whenever
there was any extraordinary Emer-
gency for making ufe of the People, as in time of War, it was always
contriv'd, that the *Oracle* fhould
be *confulted*, which never fail'd to
Pronounce in favour of the prefent
Government. No wonder then, the
Priests were fuch Favourites at *Court*,
fince they were fo ufeful to the
Prince in the Managing and Steer-
ing of the common People. We
find in Hiftory, that fome few had
the Priviledge to enter into the *San-
Ctuaries* of thefe *Oracles*, where all
the *Machines* of the *Priefts* lay ;
but they were Perfons of no lefs
Quality than *Alexander* and *Vefpafi-*
an. And the reafon why they fhew'd
this favour only to *Princes*, was
becaufe they knew it to be *their* Intereft to keep the Secret ; and that
in the Circumftances they were
then, they had much more reafon
to *raife* than to *leffen* the Reputation

of *Oracles*. And for this very reafon, the learned Men, for fear they
fhould difoblige their *Princes*, durft
not fpeak againft *Oracles*. But in
procefs of 'time, the People grew
lefs credulous of their *Priefts*, and
fo the *Oracles* were ftruck Dumb.
Hence the Learned *Selden* obferves,
That *no fooner did People ceafe
to believe* Oracles, *but even the O-*
racles *themfelves did then ceafe to
be.* So that the Occafion of their
Ceafing, was no more, than as it
is with Shop-keepers Breaking, the
lofs of Credit. But to conclude,
that which moft difcover'd the Vanity of the *Oracles*, was that even
thofe who confulted 'em (which they
did only to comply with the Weak-
nefs of the People, and gain Reputation among the unthinking Multitude) if they found them not fa-
vorable, either went on neverthelefs
in the Profecution of their Defigns,
or elfe forced them to *pronounce* fuch
as fhould be to their advantage.
This Courfe was taken by *Alexan-*
der

der the Great, and *Cleomenes* ; by the *former*, when he confulted the *Pythian* ; by the *other*, when he confulted the *Delphick* Oracle : Both which they forc'd to fay what they pleas'd themfelves. And thus I hope, I have to the Satisfaction of the Reader, demonftrated, That the *Oracles* which have made fuch a mighty noife in the World, were nothing but the Juggles and Impoftures of the *Heathen Priefts* ; and that the *Devil* was no otherwife the Author of 'em, than as he is properly faid to be the Author of all Sin and Wickednefs. What reafon then had Mr. *Edwards* to fall upon me with fo much Malice and Bitternefs of Spirit, belching out fuch Expreffions as thefe, *viz.* That *I am wonderfully Civil and Obliging, extreamly Courteous and Friendly to the great Enemy of Mankind.* And then with wonderful Smartnefs he goes on, *I fee the* Devil *is a very Innocent and Harmlefs Creature, according to fome Perfons* ; (I fancy,

without

without confulting an *Oracle*, I can
tell what he means •by the word
Some;) But now comes the *Infpi-
ration Thought, But it will be well
for them if they find it fo,* Indeed,
I thought it a thoufand Pitties, that
fo much Wit and good Nature
fhould be loft to the World, and
therefore pray let Mr. *Edwards*
have all the Praife and Honour of
it, and fo I bid him *Farewell.* Thus
in the firft Ages of the World did
Men fuffer themfelves to be gull'd
and chous'd by the Artifice of their
Crafty and Ambitious *Priefts*, whofe
only *Principle* was that of INTE-
REST.

Let us now fee whether; when
Popery came upon the Stage, the
world was any thing mended : Or,
whether the *Popifh Priefts* were men
more abftracted from *Worldly Intereft*, or no. In after times, when
Rome Pagan became *Rome Chriftian*,
then fprung there up a new *Set* of
men, who for Craft and Subtilty
did many degrees outgo their Pre-
decesfors,

deceſſors, the *Heathen Prieſts* ; theſe appear'd but meer Bunglers, Compared to this new Brood, whoſe very Religion was nothing elſe, but *Sacerdotal Intereſt.*For who ever examines the whole Fabrick of *Popery* ſhall find, That the Corner Stone of that Building is *Intereſt*, and were it not for the *Profitable* part, I queſtion not but the *Fooliſh* part of *Popery* would ſoon be laught out of Doors. But ſince the true Nature of things is beſt to be learnt in their *Minute parts* we will lay aſide *Generals*, and deſcend to *Particulars* : To begin therefore with the very *Original* of *Popery*, which you will find to be thus. As on the one hand it muſt be confeſs'd , That the *Primitive Chriſtians,*who were generally Subjects of the *Roman* Empire, had a very great Deference and Reſpect, for the Biſhops of *Rome*, becauſe that was the *Imperial* City ; ſo on the other hand , Church-Hiſtory plainly ſhews,That notwithſtanding this great Deference, the Biſhops of

Rome

Rome had no Authority or Jurisdiction out of their own *Province*, that is, beyond the *Suburbicary* Region of *Italy*, till after the Division of the *Roman* Empire into *Eastern* and *Western*. It was not long after that Division, and chiefly upon the Weakness of the *Western* Empire, that that Power, which we now call the *Papacy*, grew up. As the *Empire* decay'd, so by degrees *this* encreased and gather'd strength; the Design being at first, not to set up a *new Religion*, but a *new Monarchy* in the place of the *Old* then expiring. Thus while the *Roman* Empire was gasping for Life, did the Bishops of *Rome* force it to make what Will and Testament they pleas'd. And therefore Mr. *Hobbs* calls the *Papacy, The Ghost of the deceased* Roman *Empire, sitting Crown'd upon the Grave thereof.* Being thus Establish'd, and making *Rome* whose Name was still Venerable, the Seat of their Dominion, they soon obtain'd a Supremacy over the *Western* World.

World. In this Manner, and with these Steps did the *Papacy* first advance it self; their Designs being apparently Secular, tending not to the Salvation of Mens Souls, but the Support of their own Grandeur. And therefore these *Spiritual Machiavillians*, according to the Old Policy, are for preferving their Empire after the fame Way and Manner as it was at firft acquir'd. No wonder then, that the chief *Topick* of *Popery*, is *Argumentum ab Utili*; which of all Arguments carries the greateft force in the Church of *Rome*: And this will more plainly appear, if we do but draw up the Curtain, and prefent you with *Popery* in its full fight. 'Tis fcarce within the reach of *Arithmetick*, what vaft, prodigious Sums thefe feveral Doctrines [the *Pope's Supremacy*; *Purgatory*; *Indulgences*; *Auricular Confeffion*; and the *Celibacy* of the *Clergy*] bring in to the Church; And therefore (as one wittily expreffes it)

They

They must maintain them; because they are maintained by them.

1. To begin then with the *Pope's Supremacy.* How flight a Foundation this Doctrine hath, I think to any rational Man will foon appear; for fuppofing St. *Peter* was Bifhop of *Rome* (tho' as I fhall prove anon, there is little reafon to believe any fuch thing) and as *Metropolitan* thereof, he had the Preceedency of the reft of the Apoftles ; what then ? Could hence a fufficient Power be devolv'd on his Succeffor, to raife a real *Monarchy*, and to claim an abfolute Jurifdiction over the whole World, with a Power to difpofe of Crowns and Kingdoms ? This is certainly a *Non Sequitur.* Nor was St. *Peter* ever vefted with any fuch Priviledges as thefe, nor did his Succeffors for many Ages ever challenge 'em ; and at laft the only Title the *Pope* had to 'em, was *U-furpation.* But indeed, 'tis fo far from being demonftrable, that St. *Peter* was Bifhop of *Rome,* that it is

is not fo much as Probable he was
ever there. I am fure the *Scripture*
mentions no fuch thing ; and his
Epiftle is dated from *Babylon* in *Af-
fyria*. When *Paul* writes to the
Romans, and fends *Greeting* to a-
bove Forty by Name, he fays not
the leaft tittle of *Peter*; whom in
all probability, he would have remember'd either then, or afterward,
when from *Rome* he fent particular
Salutation from others in feveral of
his *Epiftles.* Nay, he complains,
Philipp. 2. 21. That *all who were
at* Rome, *fought their own, not the
Things which are Jefus Chrift's.* And
2 *Tim.* 4. 16. *Paul* at his firft Anfwer, when conven'd before *Nero,*
complain'd, That *no Man ftood by
him, but all Men forfook him.* All
which fure he could not have faid,
if *Peter* had been there. I know it
is generally faid, That St. *Peter* af-
fum'd the Bifhoprick of *Rome* in the
time of *Claudius*, who (as St. *Luke*
and other Hiftories do report) did
banifh all the *Jews* from *Rome*, as
Tiberius

Tiberius alſo had done before him.
And then, how can a Man reaſonably believe, That ſo skillful a *Fiſher-
man*, as St. *Peter*, ſhould chuſe to
caſt his *Net* there, where he knew,
there were no Fiſh to be caught ?
Again, I cannot conceive for what
reaſon, or to what end and purpoſe
St. *Peter*, who was an Apoſtle ſhould
be made a *Biſhop*: Methinks this is
ſo far from being neceſſary, that really to me it ſeems very prepoſterous. For by vertue of his *Apoſtle-
ſhip* he had ſufficient Power to exerciſe *Epiſcopal* Functions and Authority, either at *Rome* or any where
elſe. What need a *Soveraign Prince*
be made a *Juſtice of Peace* ? It had
therefore been a great Degradation
of St. *Peter*, and Diſparagement to
the *Apoſtolical Majeſty*, for him to
take upon him the Biſhoprick of
Rome ; juſt as if the *King* ſhould be
Lord Mayor of *London* ; or as if
the *Biſhop* of *London* ſhould be made
Vicar of *Pancras*. But how unreaſonable ſoever this Doctrine of the
Supremacy

Supremacy may appear to thofe who get not by it, yet his *Holineß*, has reafon to keep it up, fince it ferves to the filling his Coffers: And if he fhould once part with it, he at the fame time lopps off the beft Branch of his Revenue.

2. As to *Purgatory:* This Doctrine was never fo much as thought off till St. *Auftin's* time, who both *faid* it, and *unfaid* it, and at laft left it doubtful: Nor did it come into any fort of Credit till about two Hundred years after, in the time of Pope *Gregory* the Firft. The *Papifts* themfelves are fo divided as to all the Points and Circumftances of this Doctrine, that poffibly it will not a little Entertain the Reader, to fee the foolifh variety of Opinions relating to this Doctrine: *Firft* as to the *Place,* where they fuppofe this Imaginary Gaol to be ; *Eckius* will have it to be in the Bottom of the Sea ; *others* will have it either in Mount *Ætna* or *Vefuvius* ; but *Bernard de Buftis* places
ces

ces it in an Hill in *Ireland.* Next,
as to the *Torments*; Sir *Thomas More*
will have 'em to be only by *Fire* ;
but *Fisher* by *Fire* and *Water*; *Lori-
chius*, neither by Fire nor by Water,
but by the violent Convulsions of
Hope and *Fear*. Then as to the
Executioners, or *Tormentors* ; They
do as little agree about them ; for
Bishop *Fisher* will have 'em to be the
Holy Angels ; but Sir *Thomas More*
to be the very *Devils*. Then, as to
the *Sins* to be there *Expiated*; some
will have 'em to be the *Venial* only;
but others say the *Mortal* too. And
for the time of the Souls continuance
in that State, *Dennis* the *Carthusian*
extends it to the end of the World;
whereas *Dominicus à Soto* limits it
to ten years; and others make it
depend on the Number of *Masses*,
and Offices, that shall be said or
done on their behalf. Lastly, as
to the *Extremity* of the *Pains*; *A-
quinas* makes them as violent as
those of *Hell* ; but the *Rhemists*, in
their Annotations upon *Revelations*
the

the 14th, *verse* the 13th, fay, That
the Souls there are in a very fine
Condition; And *Durandus, de Offic.
Mortuorum, cap.* VII. between thefe
Extreams, gives 'em fome Intermif-
fion from thofe terrible Pains, upon
*Sundays,*and *Holy-days.* So foolifhly
extravagant are thefe feveral Fancies
& Conceits of *Purgatory,*that it may
not be altogether Impertinent to enquire into the Original and Source of
this Doctrine: And this will prefently
appear to any one who is in the leaft
vers'd in the Heathen Poets and Philofophers. *Thefe* were the firft Hatch-
ers of this Notion, and from thence
was it firft deriv'd. *Homer,* in the
fecond Book of his *Odyff.* Entertains
us with long Stories of *Ulyffes's*
Defcent into Hell; the Dialogues
of Ghofts; the Punifhment of Departed Souls; and the Sacrifices to
be Offer'd to relieve 'em: And herein is he imitated by *Virgil,* who,in
the fixth of his *Æneids,* brings in
Anchifes difcourfing at the fame rate.
Nor were their *Philofophers* free from
thefe

thefe fort of Dreams ; witnefs *Plato*, who in his Book *De Animâ* broaches the like Doctrine : and *Cicero*, in *Scipio's* Dream, Harps upon the fame String. Hence *Bellarmin* urging feveral reafons for this Doctrine of *Purgatory*, his *third* is taken from the common Opinion of all Nations, *Hebrews*, *Mahumetans*, and *Gentiles*, both *Philofophers* and *Poets*. But to conclude this Point, as ridiculous as this Doctrine of *Purgatory* is, there is not any one Opinion in the Church of *Rome*, that the *Romanifts* are more zealous in the Afferting : Nor is it to be wonder'd, that they are fo, fince herein they Act upon *Demetrius's* Principle, becaufe *thereby they have their Gain*; and therefore well may they be allow'd to be Angry, and Difpleas'd at all thofe, who fpeak or write againft it : For by that means *their Craft is in danger to be fet at nought*. There being no Opinion in their Church, which brings in a better and more conftant Revenue

Revenue, by *Maſſes, Dirges, Requiems, Trentals,* and *Anniverſaries,* beſides *Caſualties* and *Deodands,* by dying Perſons, or their Friends, in hopes of a ſpeedier Releaſe out of the Pains of *Purgatory.* So that if this Opinion were once out of Countenance in the World, they wou'd then loſe one of the beſt Arts they have of upholding the Grandure of their Church. And it is very remarkable, That the fear of loſing this Income, was one main impediment to reſtrain the Pope from yielding to a *Reformation.*

3. As to *Indulgences* and *Pardons:* In the Primitive times, when the *Chriſtians* had committed any heinous Crime, as for Example, either in denying their Faith, or Sacrificing to Idols, for fear of Perſecution ; the Parties offending were enjoyn'd ſome ſevere and long Pennance : And the rigour of this, the Biſhops, or Paſtors, in their reſpective Congregations had Power (if they ſaw Cauſe) to mitigate at their diſcretion ; which

D Mitigation,

Mitigation, or Relaxation of Punishment was call'd an *Indulgence*, or sometimes a *Pardon*. And this was deriv'd from St. *Paul*, who releas'd the *Inceſtuous Corinthian* from the Bond of Excommunication, upon his Humiliation, and ſerious Repentance. This manner of *Indulgence* was Ancient and of long Continuance in the Primitive Church. The firſt Account we have of perverting this Cuſtom, and the proſtituting it, to ſecular Ends, was in the time of Pope *Gregory* the I. about the year *Six-Hundred*. And ever ſince that time, 'tis ſcarce credible, what an immenſe Sum this Doctrine has brought in to the Church. And certainly, of all the Arts that the Church of *Rome* hath for the raiſing of *Money*, this is the clevereſt, and neateſt Contrivance ; and therefore One wittily calls theſe *Indulgences* Emulgences, and even by the *Romaniſts* themſelves they are ſtil'd, in their trueſt Signification, *The Treaſury of the Church.* The *Pope* is
the

the sole Dispenser and Disposer of these *Indulgences*; and therefore whenever he hath occasion, or a mind to fill his Treasury, all that he needs to do, is, upon pretence of War against the Infidels or Hereticks, to send out, and proclaim Marts, and Sales for these *Indulgences;* upon condition that those, who wou'd disburse any Sums of *Money* (which is all to be laid out, as he pretends, upon the said Occasion) shou'd have *Pardons* and *Indulgences* for numbers of years proportionable to the Summs they cou'd, or wou'd deposite; *Nam aliter non absolvebantur nisi tribuerent secundùm posse Suum, & facultatem Suam* ; for otherwise they cou'd not be absolv'd, except they did disburse as much as their Abilities wou'd afford, as *Henry de Knighton,* an *English* Historian in *Richard* the second's time, honestly and plainly tells us: And then as for the Poor and Indigent, truly they deserve our pity when the *Taxa Cameræ Apostolicæ,* deals thus plainly with 'em,

D 2   *Nota*

Nota diligenter quòd hujufmodi Gratiæ non conceduntur Pauperibus ; Quia non habent, ergò non poffunt Confolari ; Note diligently, *That fuch Graces are not granted to the Poor* ; Becaufe *they have not wherewithal, they cannot be comforted :* A very fad cafe indeed *!* Thus, tho' our *Saviour* tells us, how hard a thing it is for a *Rich* Man to enter into the Kingdom of Heaven, yet by the Religion of *Popery*, the difficulty lies wholly on the *Poor* Man's fide ; And the only Sin capable of *Damning* a *Rich* Man, is that of *Covetoufnefs* ; for let him but oil St. *Peter's* Keys well, and than the *Wicket* will prefently be open'd, and the Soul let into the *Popifh Heaven*, which I doubt at laft will prove but a *Fools Paradife.*

4. As to *Auricular Confeffion.* The neceffity of this Doctrine was unknown to the Fathers of the Primitive Church. Nay, about a thoufand years after *Chrift*, it was held difputable in the *Roman* Church. And

And tho' the Practice of it was im-pos'd by Pope *Innocent*, in his Coun-cil of *Lateran* ; yet even then it re-main'd difputable as to the Doctrine, till the *Council* of *Trent* gave it the Sanction of *Divine Faith.* At firft it was voluntary, and only us'd in cafe of a troubled Confcience, or a ftrong Temptation : But it is now made neceffary at ftated times, in all probability to make the *Prieft* Mafter of every Man's fecrets. This is the main curb of the *Laity*, where-by the *Clergy* hold them in awe ; for by this means they have an *In-telligencer* in the breaft of every great Man of their Communion ; which is a Thing of that vaft Confe-quence, that if ever they part with it, then farewell *Popery.*

5. As for the *Celibacy* of the *Cler-gy*. That this Cuftom was deriv'd from the *Heathens* will plainly ap-pear ; *Clemens Alexandrinus* tells us, That the *Ancient Hereticks* took occafion to condemn Marriage from the Precepts and Practices of *Pagan*

D 3   Philofophers.

Philofophers. And St. *Hieron* faith, That the *Athenian Hierophanta's* to this day, by fupping the Broth of *Hemlock*, make themfelves Chaft (being forbidden Marriage) before they were admitted into facred Orders, or advanced to *Prelatical* Dignity. And *Alexander ab Alexandro* informs us, That the *Priefts* of *Cybele* did caftrate themfelves, that they might be chaft. And he further adds in the fame place, That thofe who perform'd their greateft Solemnities (or their *Chief Priefts*) that they might continue in chaft Religion, and efcape the Contagion of Women, did emafculate themfelves with certain Herbs. And *Euripides* teftifieth, That in *Crete* thofe whom they call'd *The Prophets of Jupiter*, do not only abftain from Flefh, but alfo from all favoury Meat. And the like did the *Indian Magi*, who were advanced to the *Priefthood of the Sun*: And among the *Affyrians*, the *Priefts* of *Diana Ecbatana* liv'd in perpetual Virginity. To add more Teftimonies

monies is needlefs, fince the *Roma-nifts* are themfelves fo far from denying it, that feveral of them, as Pope *Syricius*, *Medina*, and others, urge it as an unanfwerable Argument againft the *Marriage* of *Priefts*. But notwithftanding the great care the *Heathen Priefts* took as to their *Chaftity*, yet we find it fignified but little ; and therefore *Arnobius* defcribing the fingle Life of *Priefts* amongft the *Heathen*, faith, Where are*Whoredoms* more frequently committed than by *Priefts*, even in their *Temples*, nay before the very *Altars?* And in the Conclufion he tells us, That their Luft was more frequently difcharg'd in *Chancels*, than *Brothel-Houfes*. But having fhew'd this to be a Cuftom deriv'd from the *Heathens*, and the Effect it had; Let us (now) fee, whether the *Primitive Chriftians* had any fuch Ufage; and when, and by what means, it was firft introduced, and the ufe that hath fince been made of it. That there was no fuch

Ufage

Ufage in the *Primitive Church*, is moft certain ; for St. *Ambrofe* in his *Comment* on the 2 *Cor.* 11. teftifies, That all the *Apoftles*, except St. *John* and St. *Paul*, had Wives. And alfo *Eufebius, Ruffinus*, and *Socrates*, Ecclefiaftical Writers of great Note, do all teftifie of feveral very Religious Bifhops, who had Children by their Lawful Wives, after they were Bifhops. And the *Greek* Church even to this day obferves it for a Cuftom, not to admit any into *Holy Orders*, unlefs they were *Married*; as judging them then more Staid , and lefs fubject to Temptations. The firft Account we meet with of Prohibiting *Wives* to the *Clergy*, was not long before the *Nicene Council* : A foolifh opinion had then feiz'd the Heads of fome of the leading Men of the Church, That *no Married Man was fit to Officiate at the Altar*; Whereupon the Queftion came to be ftarted in the *Council* of *Nice* ; of which matter the Ecclefiaftical Hiftorians, *Socrates,*

Socrates, lib. 1. cap. XI. gives us this Account, Ἐδόχει τοῖς ἐπισκόποις, &c. *It pleased some of the Bishops to bring in a new Law into the Church, That those who were dedicated to the Holy Ministry, viz. Bishops, Priests and Deacons, should not sleep any longer with their Wives.* But this at first was most strenuonsly oppos'd, and particularly by one *Paphnutius*, an *Ægiptian* Bishop, who had formerly one of his Eyes pluck out for the Testimony of the Blessed *Jesus.* Nor did this Doctrine advance it self into a *Decree,* till above fifty years after, at which time *Siricius* Bishop of *Rome,* first ordain'd it ; tho' for many Hundred Years after it was not much obferv'd, till *Gregory* the VII. commonly call'd *Hildebrand* began to put it in Execution ; by excommunicating all such *Marry'd Priests,* as would not immediately quit their Wives, and take the Oath of *Continency.* And this hath been strictly obferv'd ever since ; the *Council* of *Trent* having denounced an *Anathema*

ma againſt all thoſe who ſhall ſay,
That *Clerks in Holy Orders may
contract Matrimony*: *And that ſuch
a Contract is valid*, notwithſtanding
the *Laws and Conſtitutions of the
Church*. But how little this *Romiſh*
Celibacy ſignified amongſt their
Prieſts, as to the keeping 'em Chaſt,
even their own Hiſtorians can beſt
inform us. *Matthew Paris* tells us,
the *Pope* thought it almoſt a Miracle to hear a *Candidate* for a Biſhoprick atteſted to be a *pure Virgin*.
Alvarus Pelagius, a *Portugal* Biſhop,
in the 14th Century, in his known
Book, *De Planctu Eccleſiæ*, amongſt
other crying Sins of the *Roman* Clergy of his days, laments in an eſpe-
cial manner their Incontinency,
wiſhing that the *Spaniards* and *Re-
gricolæ* eſpecially, had never pro-
mis'd Continency : The Children
of the *Clergy* being in thoſe Countries (ſaith he) more numerous than
thoſe of the *Laity* ; and what is
more deteſtable, for ſeveral years
together, from their Concubines
Beds

Beds they go ftraight to the *Altar*.
And in another place, the very
fame Author complains of their de-
bauching the Women, who came
to Confeſſion. *Alphonfus à Caſtro*
tells us, That if they ſhould attempt
to conceal the Incontinency of the
Clergy, their own Children would
proclaim it. *Johannes Aventinus*
affirms, That the *Salacity* of the
Prieſts was fo famous that it was
grown into a *Proverb. Robert Holkot,*
who liv'd in the 14th Century, a
Dominican by Profeſſion and born at
Northampton, ſtiles the *Prieſts* of
his days, *Prieſts* of *Priapus* and *Ba-*
alpheor. *Johannes Gerſon,* fpeaking
of the Incontinency of the *Prieſts,*
faith, That it was fo rooted an E-
pidemical an Evil, that as, things
ſtood under the Reign of *Celibacy,*
if *Prieſts* were not allow'd the ufe
of common Women, they would
(in feveral places) turn up the Wives
and Daughters of their Pariſhioners.
Nay, even *Albertus Pighius* and *Do-*
minicus Soto, as ſtout Aſſertors as
they

they were of the *Celibacy*, yet were fo ingenious as to confefs the Lewd-nefs it occafions. Thus could I from feveral other Inftances of the like Nature, drawn from their own Hiftorians, dilate upon this Subject; As alfo, by adding the remarkable Inftances of the great *Incontinency*, or the un-Chaft *Celibate* of feveral of their *Popes* themfelves; as of *Paul* the II. *Sixtus* the IV. *Innocent* the VIII. *Alexander* the VI. *Julius* the II. *Leo* the X. *Paul* the III. *Julius* the III, &c. But I forbear this, fince raking of Dunghills is an Employment more fit for a *Scavenger*, than a *Gentleman*. That fo great Wickednefs fhould ever be practis'd amongft fuch as ferve at the *Altar*, is indeed a thing much to be lamented; but that ever any *Chriftian Church* fhould allow and approve of fuch Practices, is Matter of Aftonifhment! And yet that the Church of *Rome* does fo, is moft clear, and manifeft. Hence we find it was One of the *German* Grievances,

That

That *such Priests as were dispos'd to live chastly, and abhorred this Sin of Uncleanness,were compell'd to take Dispensations to keep Concubines.* Nicolaus *de* Clemangis also makes the same fort of Complaint; *What a strange thing is it,*says he, *That in several Dioceses now a days, the Rectors of Parishes bargain with theirBishops for License to keepConcubines?* That greatAngelicalDoctor of theChurch of *Rome,* Thomas Aquinas (whether from his own Complexion, or no, I know not) seems to be fo great a favourer of this Vice, that he argues for it in a pretty odd fort of a Manner, in his 4th Book *De Regimine Principum ; Id facit in Mundo Meretrix,*&c. *AWhore in the World,* fays he, *is as the Pump in a Ship, or a Privy in a Palace : Take these away, and all will be filled with Stench and Annoyance.* Most Incomparable Divinity ! Sure if this Rule be true , no place for sweetness can compare with *Rome,*where,by the best Computation,are reckon'd Three Thoufand

fand licens'd *Harlots*, which pay an annual Tribute to his *Holineß*. But to return to my Subject; fince it plainly appears, That this Do-ctrine of the*Celibacy* was never us'd, nor practis'd amongft the *Chriftians* of the Primitive Church, how came then this Innovation to be introdu-ced into the Church of *Rome* ; *Cui bono*? For what end and purpofe hath it fo many Ages been fo very zealoufly afferted? *In promptu Caufa eft*, The reafon is very obvious, and a Man with half an Eye may fee the Policy of it. This Doctrine then is maintained by the Policy of the *Ccurt* of *Rome*, on purpofe to make advantage of the *Clergy*, both while they live, and when they dye. Hence their great *Efpencæus* lays out fhame of that execrable Cuftom of indulging*Concubinage* to profeffers of Chaftity, at a fet annual Rate ; affuring us, That amongft the vaft Numbers of Delinquents in this kind, few, or none, fuffer any o-ther Punifhment than that of the Pocket.

Pocket. But besides this, 'tis of great advantage to his *Holiness*, to disengage the *Clergy* from all civil Interests, and thus to make 'em wholly depend upon the *Court* of *Rome*; Which is a thing cou'd never be effected, so long as the *Clergy* gave hostages of their fidelity to the Civil Government, by the. Interests of their Families and Children. And therefore this Invention was cunningly enough contriv'd; That as the old *Roman* Soldiers were forbidden Marriage while they received Pay, least their *Domestick Concerns* shou'd abate their Courage; So the *Celibacy* of the *Clergy* was strictly enjoin'd, to make 'em more true and hearty to the Interest of the *Court* of *Rome*. And the vast advantages that accrue to his Holiness by this one Doctrine of the *Celibacy* of the *Clergy*, is scarce to be computed; since now the *Church* is the general Heir to all the *Clergy*.

Thus

Thus have I run over thofe five feveral Gainful Doctrines in the Church of *Rome*; whereby it is moft manifeft, That, let 'em pretend what they will, Grandeur and Secular Intereft is all they aim at; And therefore let us no longer wonder at this *Prieft-Craft* of theirs, but rather conclude with that Ingenious *Cardinal*, who, when the People flockt about him, gave them his Benediction in thefe. Words, **Si decipi vult Populus decipiatur;** *if the People will be deceiv'd, let 'em.* Since then *Intereft* has fo great an Influence in our fpiritual Concerns, no wonder it has fo abfolute a Dominion over the *Secular* part of the World. Let People therefore talk as long as they pleafe of *Liberty, Property, Confcience,* and the like, all this is nothing but *Cant*; but the main Bufinefs and Earneft of the World is *Money, Dominion,* and *Power,* and how to compafs thofe Ends; and not a rufh Matter at laft, whether it be by *Force,* or by *Cunning,*

ning. Might and *Right* are inseparable, in the Opinion of the World; and he that has the longer Sword, shall never want, either *Lawyers* or *Divines,* to assert his Title. In a Word, he that understands Mankind aright, (that is, judging Men not as they shou'd be, but as they are, and I fear ever will be) shall find, That *Private Interest* is the string in the *Bears* Nose, it is *that* Governs the *Human Beast.* To conclude then, There's not any Corruption in Nature, but Money (another Word for *Interest*) is at one end of't ; the whole World is under the Dominion of it ; for all Things under the Sun are Bought and Sold :

Our *Iron* Age is grown an Age of
    Gold ;
'Tis who bids moft ; for all Men
    wou'd be Sold.

        D R Y D. *Amphytr.*

    E .   ESSAY II.

ESSAY II.

The great Mischief and Prejudice of
LEARNING ; *And that a Wise*
Man ought to be preferr'd before a
Man of LEARNING.

LEARNING does but
serve to fill us full of Artificial Errors. That which
we so much admire under
the Name of *Learning,* is only the
knowing the Fancies of Particular
Men, *Deliri veteris Meditantes Som-*
nia vana, in effect but like *Gossipping*
Women, telling one another their
Dreams. Most of the Pretenders to
Learning are meer *Plagiaries;* they do
but *Copy* one after another ; and me-
thinks it is but a poor easie *Knowledge*
that can be learnt from an *Index* ;
and a mean Ambition to be rich in
the Inventory of anothers Treasure.
Thus have we not seen some, even

of our *First rate* Writers, that have been better at Disguising other People's Works, than furnishing any thing of their Own ;_ That is to say, upon the taking them to pieces, the *Stuff* and *Trimming* is found to be wholly stolen, and new Furbish'd ; and, Nothing (in short) that they can assume to themselves, but the *Needle* and *Thread* that tackt the *Composition* together. Many (therefore) who affect to be thought Men of *Learning,* may very properly be compar'd to *Æsop's Daw,* which is a true *Type* of a *Plagiary* ; for he makes himself fine with the Plunder of all Parties. He is a *Smuggler* of *Wit,* and steals Fancies without paying the Customary Duties. Whatever he Writes, may properly be call'd his *Manufacture* ; for it is more the Labour of his *Finger* than his *Brain.* In short, There is not a simpler Animal, and a more superfluous Member of a State than a *meer Scholar* : He is *Telluris inutile Pondus.* And were I to give a description of a *Pedant,*

newly

newly arriv'd from the *University*, I cou'd not do it. more to the Life, than in the Words of *Horace* :

Cùm Septem Studijs annos dedit,
    inf●uitq;
Libris & Curis, Statuâ taciturnior
    exit
Plerumq; & ●ulum risu qua-
    tit.———

No wonder then, that the *Itali-ans*, in their *Farces*, always bring in a *Pedant* for the Fool of the Play.

The *Romans* also were so far from esteeming *Learning*, as an essential part of Wisdom, that with them the Word *Scholar* was seldom us'd but by way of Reproach. That *Learning* is no way serviceable to the Life of Man, even daily experience sufficiently shews; for how many are there in the World, of high and low Condition, that live pleasantly and happily, who never trouble themselves with *Learning*. Neither is it
                            serviceable

serviceable to things Natural, which
an ignorantSot may as well perform,
as he that is vested with the greatest
Learning ; Nature is a sufficient Mistress for that.   Nor doth it conduce to honesty, and to make us
Better ; *Paucis est Opus literis ad bo-
nam Mentem* , little Learning is requisite for a good Mind : Nay, some
are of Opinion, it rather hinders it ;
And that where *Learning* and Knowledge go in the *Front*, Pride and Ambition always follow in the *Rear*.
Hence it is observ'd, That *Rome* for
the first five hundred Years, when
it flourish'd in Virtue and Valour,
was without *Knowledge* ; but as soon
as *Learning* came amongst them, they
then began to degenerate, and to
run into Factions.   The best establish'd Government that ever was,
and from whence have Sprung the
greatest Personages in the World, I
mean the *Lacedemonian*, did in no
sort pretend to *Learning* : And yet
it was the School of Virtue and
Wisdom, and was ever Victorious

over *Athens,* the most *Learned* City
of the World, the School of all
Science, the Habitation of the Muses, and the Storehouse of Philosophers. *Learning* then serves for nothing, but to invent Niceties and
Subtilties, artificial cunning Devices,
and whatsoever is an Enemy to Vertue and Innocence. Atheism, Errors,
Sects, and all the Troubles of the
World, have risen from the Men of
Knowledge and *Learning* : 'Tis *Learning,* I say, which has enabled them
for those Quirks and Subtilties, of
which grosser Understandings wou'd
have remain'd more happily ignorant. If we search into the *Morals*
of the most *Learned* amongst the
Heathens, I mean their *Philosophers,*
we shall find but little agreement betwixt their Practices and their Doctrines. And that the one did generally run counter to the other.
Plutarch tells us, That not only
Socrates and *Plato,* but also the rest
of the *Philosophers,* notwithstanding
their outward shew and ostentation

of

of fome Vertues, were generally as Intemperate, Incontinent, and Wicked, as any common or ordinary Slave. We are likewife told from very good Authority, That *Ariftotle* did by no means live up to the Rule of his own *Ethicks*; as being guilty of great Vanity in his Clothes, of Incontinency, and Unfaithfulnefs to his Mafter *Alexander*, &c. Nay, what fhall we fay, if our great *Seneca*, that Man of *Morals*, had his Vices and Enormities? Whom notwithftanding St. *Jerom* would have Canoniz'd for a *Saint*; yet if what *Dion Caffius* and other Authors of Note, fay of him be true, I am fure he did but little deferve it. We contemn, fays *Minutius Felix*, the proud Looks of the *Philofophers*, whom we have known to be Corrupters of Youth (or *Sodomites*) and *Adulterers*, and *Tyrants*, and always eloquent againft their own Vices. *Grotius* in his *Annotations* on *Ephef.* 5. v.6. informs us, That the Sin of *Sodomy* was generally allow'd by

E 4 the

the *Philosophers*. And the same Author on 1 *Cor.* 5.2, assures us, That
both the *Cynicks* and *Stoicks* judged
Incest amongst their Αδιαφορα, *Things
Indifferent.* Thus we see notwithstanding the specious Pretentions, &
affected Gravity of these *musty Mo-
ralists*, the *Antient Philosophers*, their
Lives were no way correspondent
to their Doctrines, nor did their
Practises hold an equal pace with
their *Theory.* ———— *Video melio-
proboque ; Deteriora sequor.* We naturally know what is *good*, but naturally pursue what is *Evil*. And as
the *Philosophers* were defective in
their *Morals* ; so I do not find, they
had any great Stock of solid Learning. St. *Aust* tells us in his *Epist*.
131. That all the Knowledg and
Learning of the *Philosophers*, was nothing else but jangling Sophistry,
Towers built in the Air, proud Error and curious Lies. We may easily gather from *Tully* and *Laertius*,
what a small Proportion of solid
Learning these *Philosophers* were Masters

sters of; Their Controversies were infinite, their Dissentions endless, and irreconcileable, about no less Matters than the *Soveraign* and *Chief Good*, nay and about *God* himself; holding concerning the *first*, 288 several Opinions, and 300 about the *latter*. Many of their *Summum Bonums* that they presented us with, were only fit to entertain a *Brute*, tho others indeed were noble enough for a Spirit of the highest Order. I could not tell where to stop should I relate the Differences one Sect had with another, their Inconsistences with themselves, and the ridiculous and ill supported *Tenets* some of the most famous of them have held. And therefore well might *Tully* observe, as he did, That there was scarce any Opinion in Nature so gross, absurd, or ridiculous, but was asserted and maintain'd by some *Philosopher* or other. 'Tis to be confess'd, *They* had a great Command of Words, and withal a good Stock of Assurance, and so were better able to *Harangue*

and

and *Dispute* it , than the common
People ; they could talk more plau-
fibly about that they did not un-
derstand ; but still their *Learning* lay
chiefly in Flourish, and Terms, and
Cant ; for as for any real Improvements in Science , they were not
much wiser than the less pretending
Multitude. But after I have said this,
I can by no means deny, but that
some of these *Philosophers* were
Men of excellent Wits , and great
Natural Parts ; yet, I say, the way
they took was not like to bring
much Advantage to *Knowledg*, or a-
ny of the Uses of *Humane Life* ;
being for the most part that of *Notion* and *Dispute* , which still runs
round in a *Labyrinth* of *Talk*, but
advanceth nothing. It was a most
perverse Custom amongst the *Disci-
ples* of the Ancient *Philosophers,*
not to make any *strict Choice* ; to
leave some and embrace others of
their Masters Doctrines, but to swallow all at once. Thus he that became a *Stoick,* an *Epicurean,* a *Peri-
patetick,*

patetick, in *Logic,* or *Moral Philoso-*
phy,or *Physicks* ; never ftuck prefently to affent to whatever his
Founder had faid in all the other
Sciences ; tho there was no kind of
Connexion between his Doctrine in
the *one* and the *other.* Thus was the
whole Image of *Philofophy* form'd
in their Minds altogether : And
what they receiv'd fo carelefly,they
defended the fame way; not in par-
cels,but in grofs. No wonder then,
fince they took this unadvifed Method, that they often flipt into fuch
grofs Errors and Miftakes. Hence
therefore, if we look back into the
firft Ages of the Church, we fhall
find,That *Philofophy* was the chief
Seminary of the main Errors broach'd
in thofe times. And this (no doubt)
Tertullian was highly fenfible of,
which made him ftyle the *Philofo-*
phers, the *Patriarchs* of *Hereticks.*
And *Cornelius Agrippa* fays , That
nothing more adulterates *Divinity*
than *Philofophy*; forafmuch as all
Herefy whatfoever hath had it's
firft

firſt Riſe out of the Fountain of
Philoſophy. The Primitive Fathers
of the Church, were wont to apply
themſelves with great diligence to
the Study of Heathen *Philoſophy*, on
purpoſe to enable them to fight the
Heathens with their own Weapons,
and to baffle them with their own
Arguments. Whereupon they chiefly
conſulted the *Philoſophy* of *Ariſtotle*
and *Plato* ; but chiefly *Plato*'s; becauſe that ſeem'd to ſpeak plainer
about the *Divine Nature*; and alſo,
becauſe the Sweetneſs and Power-
fulneſs of *Plato*'s Writings, taught
'em at the ſame time the Art of
Speaking, and the Strength of Rea-
ſoning. Having thus provided themſelves againſt their Adverſaries, they
eaſily got the Victory over them ;
For tho the *Heathens* for ſo many
hundred Years, had very zealouſly
aſſerted the Truth of their ſeveral
Religions ; yet now their *Philoſophers* were ſo baffl'd by theſe *Chriſtian Doctors*, that they had nothing
to ſay ; and at laſt were ſo ingenious,

nious, as to confeſs the ridiculouſ-
neſs of *their* Religions, and to own
the purity and reaſonableneſs of the
Chriſtian Worſhip. And now, after
ſo good a Beginning, who could
expect ſo unhappy a Concluſion?
For it ſo fell out, That the *Chriſti-*
ans having had ſuch good Succeſs
againſt the Religions of the *Hea-*
thens, by their own Weapons; inſtead of laying them down when
they had done, unfortunately fell to
manage them one againſt another.
So many ſubtle Brains having been
ſet on work, and heated againſt a
Foreign Enemy; when that was o-
ver, and they had nothing elſe to do
(like an Army that returns victorious, and is not preſently disbanded)
they began to ſpoyl and quarrel a-
mongſt themſelves. Hence that Religion, which at firſt appear'd ſo innocent and peaceable, and fitted for
the Benefit of Human Society, was
miſerably divided into a thouſand
intricate Queſtions, which neither
advance true Piety, nor good Manners,

ners. And from hence fprung up the
firft *Herefies* in the Church. I know
it was the Policy of *Julian* to fhut
up the Fountains of *Human Learn-*
ing from the *Chriftian Iouth*, leaft
they fhould by that means become
Mafters of fuch acutenefs, as might
render them the more formidable
Adverfaries to *Paganifm* : But cou'd
he have forefeen, that they would
have employ'd thofe Weapons, not
fo much againft the common Enemy, as one againft another ; he
would furely have revers'd the Stra-
tagem, and freely have open'd thofe
Magazines, whence they might fur-
nifh themfelves for their mutual Ru-
in, and have as folicitoufly promoted
their *Learning*, as ever he obftructed
it. And thus we fee how little *Re-*
ligion is promoted, or advantag'd by
Human Learning, which the Apoftle
fufficiently inculcates , when he fo
wifely advifes us, *to avoid all vain*
Philofophy.

And as *Learning* is of little Ufe
in making Men truly *Religious* ; fo

it

it likewife fignifies but little in the
making us either good *Subjects,* or
great *Politicians.* *Licinius* and *Va-*
lentinian, Emperors of *Rome,* were
wont to fay, That their State had no
Poyfon more dangerous than that
of *Learning:* *Lycurgus* alfo feem'd
to be of the fame opinion, when he
eftablifht Ignorance in his Republic.
Moft Men do attribute the Greatnefs of the *Grand Seigneur's,* and the
Duke of *Mufcovy's* Power over their
Subjects, to this one fingle piece of
Policy, viz. Their fuppreffing of *Li-*
terature. And do we not fee here in
England, That, in time of *Popery,*
when that little Stock of *Learning*
that was amongft us, was cloifter'd
up in Monafteries and Abbeys, the
ignorant Common People patiently
crouch'd, and readily bore whatfoever burden was put upon 'em. But
as foon as ever Learning peept a-
broad in the World, and began to
diffufe it felf, amongft the *Vulgar* :
They then began to expoftulate
with their Superiors, and immediately

ately threw off that Yoke, which formerly they and their Fore-fathers had so long lain under. And indeed upon this Consideration it is, that Princes take so much Care to keep their Subjects in Ignorance, by suppressing all such Books, as lay open and prostitute the *Arcana Imperii* to the Knowledg of the Vulgar. For Books give Men new Hints and Notions, and those Notions do often put Men upon such Actions, as are not always agreeable to the Interests of Princes. Hence that subtle and crafty Prince, King *James* (I mean the *First*, not the *Second*) would often say, That *of all sorts of Subjects the Thinking Man made the Worst.* And even by daily Experience we find it confirm'd, That the High-flown *Arbitrary* Men (commonly the Darlings of Tyrants) are not Men of the deepest Thoughts, nor of the greatest Foresight and Consideration; since if they were, they might easily discover, That the Absolute Power of the Prince cannot

be

be made up of any other Ingredient,
than the Slavery of the Subject.
Whereas in all Great and Noble Souls
(*Queîs Meliore luto finxit præcordia
Titan*) there is an inbred Love to Liberty *:* And certainly they work by
a wrong *Engine*, who seek to gain
their *Ends* by Constraint. The crossing two *Lovers* knits but their Affection the Stronger, and makes it
burn with the greater Heat. You
may stroke the *Lion* into tameness,
but you shall sooner hew him into
pieces, than *beat* him into a Chain.
I have known several, whom the
greatest Importunity could never
prevail with to take up their Glass,
when at the same time, give 'em but
their *Liberty*, and they would be the
first Men drunk in the Company.
In short, the noblest Weapon wherewith *Man* can conquer, is Love and
Good Nature. For, generally Speaking, 'tis with *Men*, as 'tis with
Trouts, the surest way to *take* 'em,
is to *tickle* 'em. In a Word, 'tis *Liberty* alone which inspires Men with

F   Lofty

Lofty Thoughts, and elevates their Souls to the highest pitch : Whereas a Man that is under any Restraint, and in a State of Dependency, has presently a Damp struck upon his Genius, his Thoughts are overaw'd, and the range of his Fancy totally disorder'd.   And for this reason it was, That *Parmenio* could not rise up to *Alexander's* Height of *Thinking*, because he was under his Command.   'Tis *Longinus's* Observation, That there were no considerable *Orators* in *Greece* after their Government was alter'd by the *Macedonians* and *Romans.* According to *him*, their *Elocution* and their *Freedom* seem'd to languish and expire together. When they were once *enslav'd*, the *Muses* scorn'd to keep 'em Company any longer.   Thus then we find, That we cannot continue long in the Condition of *Slaves*, but we must degenerate into the Habits and Temper that is natural to that Condition, Our Minds will grow low with our Fortune, and by being accustomed

med to live like *Slaves,* we shall become unfit to be any thing else :
Etiam fera Animalia si clausa teneas
virtutis obliviscuntur, says *Tacitus,*
The fierceft Creatures by long Con-
ftraint, lofe their Courage. And I
remember, 'tis the Obfervation of
that noble Author, Sir *Francis Ba-*
con, That the Bleffing of *Iffachar,*
and that of *Judah,* falls not upon
one People, to be *Affes* crouching
under *Burthens,* and at the fame
time to have the Spirit of *Lions.*
And with their *Courage* 'tis no wonder if they lofe their *Fortune,* as
the *Effect* with the *Caufe,* and act
as ignominioufly abroad, as they
fuffer at home. *Machiavel* obferves,
That the *Roman* Armies that were
always victorious under *Confuls* ; all
the while they were under the Slavery of the *Decemviri* never profper'd. And certainly, People have
reafon to fight but faintly, where
they are to gain the Victory a-
gainft themfelves, when every fuc-
cefs fhall be a Confirmation of their

Slavery, and a new link to their Chain. Since therefore *Liberty* is a thing so highly valued by Mankind, and in all Ages has been so; no wonder then, that the wisest *Princes* have been for granting to their Subjects the greatest *Liberty*; allowing them even the freedom to speak whatever they had a mind to. And this was so far from being any prejudice to the *Prince*, that it was really the greatest Advantage imaginable to him. *Augustus Cæsar*, one of the Happiest and Greatest *Princes* that the Sun ever saw, when he was told at any time, That even his own Person and *Edicts* were too boldly discours'd of in *Rome*, was wont to say, *In Civitate liberâ linguas quoque Civium liberas esse oportere* : That in a free State or City, Mens Discourses ought also to be free, and without Restraint. And this Candid Profession of his, might possibly be no mean Ingredient in the Composition of his own Felicities. *Thuanus* writing to the great

great *Henry* the 4th of *France,* unto other Praifes of that *Prince's* Reign, adds this, as none of the meaneft, *ea eft, Domine, rara tuorum temporum fælicitas, in quibus unicuique fentire qnæ velit, & quæ fentiat eloqui licet*: Such (Grear Sir) is the rareHappinefs of your Times, that in them every Man may think what he pleafes, and fpeak what he thinks. And of the fameComplexion was that Serene Age, in which theExcellentEmperour*Trajan* reign'd as *Cornelius Tacitus* (who was then living) affirms, from whom the faid *Thuanus* feems to have borrowed the very individual Words before recited. TheLord*Bacon* very wifely noteth, that fuch*Liberties* do oftentimes give vent and difcharge to Popular Difcontentments ; and befides, the *Prince* is thereby inftructed in what part the *Subject* is pinch'd, and griev'd, when perhaps he fhall attain this Information no other Way. And to the fameEffect does the learned *Selden* tell us, That tho' fome

F 3   make

make flight of *Libels*, yet you may
fee by them how the Wind fits ;
as take a Straw, and throw it up
into the Air, you shall fee by *that*
which way the Wind is ; which you
shall not do by cafting up a *Stone*.
In fhort, *faith he*, more Solid things
do not shew the Complexion of the
Times fo well, as *Lampoons* and
Libels.   But as valuable as *Liberty*
is to moft Men, yet in fome tempers there is fuch a Natural Love to
Servitude and Vaffallage, that they
think no pleafure Comparable to the
Hugging of their Chain ; and with
the Slavifh *French Man*, their greateft Glory is, *Noftre Roy eft Abfolu*,
the Grammatical conftruction whereof is, *We are Slaves*.   But, God be
thanked, this is not the Character
of our Country-men ; They have
ftill known better things : For never was any Nation under the Sun
more tenacious of their Properties,
and by Confequence greater Affer-
ters of their *Liberties* than the *Eng-*
lifh, and that even in the moft bigotted

gotted Times of *Popery.* And nothing can be a greater Teſtimony of the Truth hereof, than the great Care our *Anceſtors* took in defending that inviolable Bulwark of our *Liberties* and *Properties,* the 𝕸𝖆𝖌= 𝖓𝖆 𝕮𝖍𝖆𝖗𝖙𝖆, or 𝕲𝖗𝖊𝖆𝖙 𝕮𝖍𝖆𝖗𝖙𝖊𝖗 of *England* ; a *Charter* purchaſt with the *Treaſures,* and ſeal'd with the *Bloud* of our *Anceſtors.* A *Law* promulg'd and eſtabliſht to the *Engliſh,* with a Terror and Solemnity, inferiour only to *that* of the *Holy Commandments* by God himſelf to the *Jews.* There was here no *Thunder* or *Lightning* it's true ; but there was ſo dreadful a Fulmination of Curſes upon the Violaters thereof, that no Man ever yet conſider'd them without Horror and Aſtoniſhment. A *Law* rever'd by former *Parliaments* to that Degree, that they enaſted Tranſcripts thereof to be carefully preſerv'd in all the *Cathedrals* of the Realm : That it ſhould be four times a year publickly read before the People. That twice in the Year the *Prelacy* ſhould

Thun-

Thunder out the greater Excommunication againſt, the Infringers thereof. That the Lord *Chancellor,* and all the great Miniſters of State, upon entry into their Offices, ſhould conſtantly be Sworn to the Obſervation thereof. Nay that the *Prieſts* and *Confeſſors* ſhould frame the Conſciences of the People to the Obſervance thereof. And Laſtly, a *Law* confirm'd by no leſs than Thirty Two ſeveral Acts of Parliament. And (now) what was the Reaſon of all this *Veneration* and *Carefulneß*? Was this **Charter** of that *Sanctity* and *Importance*? Yes ſurely, This *Bulwark* was then thought as neceſſary to the *Engliſh,* as that of the *Palladium* to the *Trojans,* the *Holy Ark* to the *Hebrews,* or the *Sea-Banks* to the State of *Holland.* In Company of this *Tutelar,* there could be no Danger ; and in the Abſence thereof, there could be no Safety. Such *then* was the Care of our *Anceſtors,* in the fencing about of their *Rights* and *Properties.* And ſo invincible was their Zeal to tranſ-

mit

mit thefe *Jewels* to their Pofterities,
with the fame *Luftre* and *Beauty*,
that they themfelves had receiv'd
them from their Predeceffors. Thefe
old *Englifh Heroes* feeming to me
to bear always in mind that Gallant
faying of *Galaacus*, (our Countrey
Man and a great Captain) when his
Army was in the Inftant of joyning
Battle here with the *Roman* Invaders :
*Et Majores veftros, & Pofteros Co-
gitate*; 𝕱𝖊𝖑𝖑𝖔𝖜 𝕾𝖔𝖑𝖉𝖎𝖊𝖗𝖘, faith
he, 𝕽𝖊𝖒𝖊𝖒𝖇𝖊𝖗 𝖞𝖔𝖚𝖗 𝕬𝖓𝖈𝖊𝖘𝖙𝖔𝖗𝖘,
𝖆𝖓𝖉 𝕻𝖔𝖘𝖙𝖊𝖗𝖎𝖙𝖎𝖊𝖘. An Expreffion
fo weighty and fignificant, that, if
it were poffible, it ought to be
Writ with a Quill drawn from the
Wing of a *Cherubim*. And now,
that ever any who call themfelves
Englifh Men, fhould fink into fuch
a meannefs of Spirit, fo degenera-
ting from the Virtues of their *Anceftors*, as to give up at one Breath
our *Englifh Liberties*, is that, which
as our Forefathers could never have
dreamt of; fo, for the Honour of
the prefent Age, I hope Profterity
will never remember. But Monfters

are the ... ... very Age; and there is no Climate without some Insects. Tho *Liberty* (as I have said) be the Mistress of all generous Souls, and is that alone which gives a Relish to Human Life : yet, I say, there hath been lately found amongst us a sort of *Animals* who have been as Industrious in giving up, as ever our Noble Progenitors were in establishing our *Liberties*. But whatsoever Charms, these the more Gross, and earthly part of Mankind, may think there is in such a Lazy, slavish Subjection ; yet to Men of more refined Intellectuals, and whose Veins run with a Nobler Sort of Blood, all that the World can give without *Liberty* hath no Tast. It must be confess'd, That in the two last Reigns, this precious *Jewel* of *Liberty*, hath been little valued ; nothing hath been Sold so Cheap by *Unthinking* Men : But alass that doth no more lessen the real value of it, than the Ignorance of the Foolish *Indians* did that of their

their *Gold*; which at firſt they ex-
chang'd for the moſt inconſiderable
Bawbles. 'Tis the Happineſs of our
Conſtitution, That *King* and *People*
are both bounded ; and Curſt be the
Man, who ſhall go about to remove
either of theſe Land Marks : The
Crown hath *Prerogative* enough to
protect our *Liberties* ; and the *People* have ſo much *Liberty*, as is neceſſary to make them uſeful to the
Crown: So that the King's *Prerogative*, and the Subjects *Liberty*, do
naturally tend to the Preſerving one
another : It was the Obſervation of
that learned Attorney General, Sir
Francis Bacon, That whileſt the
Prerogative runs within its ancient
and proper Banks, the main Channel thereof is ſo much the ſtronger ;
for Over-flows evermore hurt theRi-
ver.

Certainly, it was no ill ſaying of
Pliny the younger, to *Trajan* the
Emperour, *Fælicitatis eſt poſſe quan-
tum velis, Magnitudinis velle quan-
tum poſſis*, It is an Happineſs for your
Majeſty

Majesty to be able to do what you will, but your Greatness confists in doing what you justly may. And *Comines* (that Honest *French* States-Man) notes, That it is more Hoourable for a *King* to say, *My Subjects are so Good and Loyal as to deny me nothing*; than to say, *I take what I please, and I will keep it.* And those Courtiers that preach any other Doctrin, do not a little mistake the Interest of their Masters, and are so far from exalting their Grandeur and Prerogative, that they make 'em indeed no Kings. For, as *Bracton* says, *Non est Rex ubi dominatur Voluntas* ; It is not a King, where Will and Pleasure bears Sway; but rather some *Cyclopick Monster* , which eats and drinks the Flesh and Blood of Mankind. Nay, even King *James* the I. (that high Afferter of Prerogative) in his Speech in the Star-Chamber , *Anno* 1609. saith, That no sooner does a King give over Governing according to *Law*, but he ceases to be a *King*, and degenerates

rates into a *Tyrant*. And the Lord Chancellor *Bacon* tells us, That the People of this Kingdom love the *Laws* thereof, and nothing will oblige 'em more, than a Confidence of the free enjoying them. What the *Lords* upon an Occaſion once ſaid, **Nolumus Leges Angliæ Mutari,** we will not have the *Laws* of *England* alter'd, is imprinted upon the Hearts of all *Engliſh Men*, who take themſelves to have as good a Title to their *Laws*, as to the Common Air they breath in. And therefore Sir *Walter Raleigh* (a Man of no Vulgar Obſervations) tells us a great Thing, and in no wiſe to be ſlighted, That *the Kings of England have evermore ſuſtained more Loſs by one Rebellion, than by a hundred years Obſervance of* **Magna Charta.** 'Tis obſerv'd of the *Camel*, that it lies quietly down till it hath its full Load, and then riſeth up ; but the *Engliſh Mobile* is a kind of *Beaſt*, which riſeth up ſooneſt, when it is over-loaden. And therefore

therefore (to Conclude this Point)
as an *English Monarch* may (so long
as he observes the *Laws*) be the Happiest Prince in the World ; so if he
will turn *Phaeton*, and drive furiously, he will in the end find himself a King not of *Men*, but of De-
vils.   And this brings to my Mind
the Observation of a great Man, *viz.*
That that which had in all Ages
kept the *English* so Free a People,
and from being Enslav'd like some
of their Neighbouring Nations,
was (next to Gods particular Goodnefs) that natural Churlishnefs,
and Roughnefs of Temper, which
is inherent in a true right *English*
Man. This Character may (poffibly)
feem to bear a little ha   upon
us : But let us fet the *Good* againft
the *Bad*, and for my part I think
(if from so bad a *Cause* we have
found fo good an Effect) we have
no reafon to Repine, but be Thank-
ful.   And befides who knows but
the fame Obfervation may hold true
in *Men*, which is in *Metals*, That
those

thofe of the ftrongeft and nobleft
Subftance, are hardeft to be Polifht.
But begging Pardon for this long
Digreffion, I fhall now proceed.

That Men of *Learning* are not
always the Greateft *Politicians,* even
the Experience of all Ages does fufficiently fhew; That great and learned Antiquary Mr. *Selden* informs
us, That when *Conftantine* became
Chriftian, He had fo great an Affection for the *Clergy,* that he put
good part of the Civil Government
into their Hands ; but after three or
four years Experience, he was very
fenfible how fatal this Error had
like to have been : Whereupon he
took new Meafures; and in the
Pofts of thefe unhappy *Politicians,*
he was fain to put in a fet of
Lay-Men, who having truer and
better Notions of Government,
foon corrected, and amended *Their*
Errors and Miftakes. That the
Clergy of *England* have fince the
Reformation been much abridg'd
of their former Power, is what I
think

think every Man will grant. And
therefore, that such of 'em as love
to be Great and Powerful, have still
a hankering after that old Constitution, I, for my part, cannot so much
admire. But how comes it, that
the *Clergy* are not *now* allow'd to
have as great Power, as in times of
Popery? The reason is very apparent;
because we found by Experience,
That when they were vested with
such great Power, no sort of Men
ever carried it more Arbitrarily, and
Tyrannically, nor (indeed) committed greater Solecisms in *Politicks*
than they did: And therefore the
History of those times does sufficiently warn us against runing into the
same Error. When Men act out of
their own Sphere, who can expect
any good will come of it? Hence
we find, it seldom happens, That
the *States Men* are more Fortunate
in medling with Religion, than the
Church Men with State-Affairs. They
both mar all with Tampering out
of their Province. *Christ's* Kingdom

dom is not of this World; nor
ought the Divines αεσγμαπυἕν, to
meddle in this *Political* · Province ;
and when they do, God knows no
fort of Men proves fo Unfortunate.
Let us hear what the Ingenious *An-
drew Marvel* fays, as to this Point.
" Whether it be, that the Clergy
" are not fo well fitted by Education,
" as others for Political Affairs, I
" know not ; tho' I fhould rather
" think (*faith he*) they have advan-
" tage above others, and if they ,
" wou'd but keep to their Bibles,
" might make the beft Minifters of
" State in the World ; yet 'tis gene-
" rally obferv'd, That Things mif-
" carry under their Government.
" If there be any Counfel more pre-
" cipitate, more violent, more rigo-
" rous, more extream than other,
" that is *theirs*. Truly I think, the
" reafon, God does not blefs 'em in
" Affairs of State, is becaufe he ne-
" ver intended 'em for that Employ-
" ment. Or, if Government, and
" the Preaching of the Gofpel, may

G   " well

" well concur in the same Per-
" son, God therefore frustrates him,
" because, tho' knowing better, he
" seeks and manages his Greatness
" by the lesser and meaner Max-
" ims.

Upon these therefore, and such
like Considerations, the Wise *Venetians* have so slight an Opinion of
the *Politicks* of their Church Men,
that whenever any thing that is of a
considerable Nature, occurs to be
debated in the *Senate*, before any
suffrage passeth, they cause Procla-
mation to be made, for all *Priests*
to depart : And the proper Officer,
with a loud and audible Voice,
pronounceth these Words, *Fuora I
Preti, Out Priests.* And it is further
Remarkable, That he who in this
Common-Wealth is call'd the *Divine of the State* (an Ecclesiastical
Person to be advis'd with in Matters
of Religion) is commonly chosen
such a One, as is reputed the least
addicted to *Bigottry.* It is the general Observation of the most Faithful

ful Historians, That the *Clergy* in
all Ages have been the greatest Promoters of those civil Distempers and
Contentions, that have every where
shak'd the Foundations of *Church*
and *State* ; so that as a *Catholick*
noted, There hath been no Floud
of Misery, but did spring from, or
at least was much swell'd by their
Holy Water. Those *Torches* that
should have been for saving Light,
have still degenerated into Fire-
brands ; those *Trumpets* that shou'd
have founded Retreats to Popular
Furies have never known any other
Musick than *Martial All-Arms.*
But God defend our *Pulpits* from
such *Boutefeus*, as like *Ætna* and
Vesuvius belch out nothing but
Flames and Fiery Discourses. Certainly, if these Men ever think to
merit Heaven, it must be by an
Antiperistasis. But in a Word, when
the Men of the *long Robe* have once
preach'd the People to *Tinder*, the
least Spark then sets 'em on Fire.
And therefore, let any Man but read

the

the History of *Christendom,* and he
will find, that most of the Quarrels
in this part of the World have sprung
from the *Pulpit,* and that the *Clergy*
were the *Porcupisces* that portended
the Storm.   That no sort of Men
have prov'd more fatal in their Counsels to Princes than the *Political
Divines,* is a truth too much confirm'd, by Experience to be deny'd.
That which these Men cheifly aim
at, is to render themselves acceptable at Court ; as knowing that the
best Preferments come from thence ;
and therefore, If they can but footh
and please the *Prince,* they value not
whether their Doctrin be true, or
false.   Hence then their chief business is, to give a helping hand towards making the *Prince* Arbitrary :
And their way to do this, is by En-
titling him to all those *Regalia's* or
*Prerogatives,*that the Kings of *Juda,*
or *Israel,* ever enjoy'd, or usurp'd ;
as if the *Judicials* of *Moses* were
calculated for all Seasons , and all
Meridians.   And thus arose that
                                          Doctrin,

Doctrin, That *Monarchy* is *Jure Divino*. But this way of Proceeding is no new Invention, for we find it very ufual amongft the Ancient *Heathens*, whenever they had a. mind to obtrude any odd Belief upon the Common People, they prefently trumpt up a *Jus Divinum* ; and after this manner we fee both their *Laws* and *Religions* were eftablifht. Thus *Solon's* Laws were faid to come from *Minerva*; *Lycurgus* deriv'd his Laws from *Jupiter* ; *Numa Pompilius*, the firft Founder of the *Roman* Rites and Ceremonies, declar'd he receiv'd them from the Goddefs *Ægeria* ; and *Mahomet* pretended his Religion was imparted to him, by the Angel *Gabriel.* There is not any thing whatfoever, that derives fo great an Authority amongft Men, as the Opinion of Divine Favour, or Heavenly Defignation : And therefore St. *Auftin* fpeaking of that Cuftom amongft the *Heathen*, of deriving the Pedigree of their *Heroes* from the Gods,

fays,

says, He lookt upon it to be of great use; in as much as it had made Valiant Men, fancying themselves to be Heaven-born, upon the confidence thereof, to undertake high Attempts the more boldly, intend them the more earnestly, and accomplish them the more succesfully. And *Ludovicus Vives* says, That another great Advantage which accrued to the *Heroes* by this Beleif, was, the Readiness which hereupon they found in the Common People to submit to whatsoever they commanded, as thinking their very Commands to be Sacred and Divine. This therefore made *Scipio*, that he cultivated and improved that Opinion of the People, *viz.* That he was begot by some *God*; and *Alexander* in *Lucian* tells us, That it further'd him in many great Designs, to be accounted the Son of *Jupiter Hammon*; for thereby he was fear'd, and none durst Oppose him, whom they held to be a *God*. Thus we see, That that Piece of Policy,

Policy, which many of our Court-Flatterers in the late Reigns have been fo fond off, *viz.* Their afferting *Monarchy* to be *Jure Divino*, is but borrw'd from this old *Heathen* Cuftom ; the Original Défign whereof was, *firft*, to flatter the Prince , by making him Believe, his Power was abfolute, and his Will was uncontrolable; and the ntoimpofe upon the *People*, by making them believe, That a Prince (tho a Tyrant, and the very Worft of Men) was not to be oppos'd, or refifted. But from what I have now faid, let no-Man think I am an Enemy to *Monarchy* ; for I do moft folemnly, and unfeignedly Declare, That of all Sorts of Governments, *Monarchy* is the moft agreeable to my Genius ; and that of *Monarchy* the *Pure* and *Unmixt* would pleafe me beft (it being *that* by which the *Almighty* governs the*Univerfe*)cou'd human Nature be long trufted with it ; and cou'd we be as certain, that his *Vicegerent* on Earth, wou'd as

eafily

easily imitate those Divine Attributes of *Wisdom* and *Goodness*, as they are prone to lay Claim to his other Attributes of *Power* and *Greatness.* But alass, *Kings* are but *Men*; they are not exempted from Error: They have their Vices and Infirmities, their Sallies and Enormities, like the rest of Mankind : And indeed, considering the unhappiness of their Education, and their being continually surrounded with *Sycophants,* and Flatterers, 'tis a wonder they prove at the common rate of other Men. Hence therefore that great Man of Wisdom and Experience, *Phillip de Comines,* tells us, That a *Vertuous Prince is worthy of more than ordinary applause.* Thus then, the fault is not in the *Government* as *Absolute,* but in *humane Nature ,* which is not often found Sufficient, at least for above one or two Successions, to support and manage so unlimited a Power in one single Person as it ought to be. And now to return to my Subject.

Since

Since *Learning* therefore is a thing of so little Value, and Use to Mankind, as we have made it appear to be; how Vain are Those, who extol it to such a Degree, as to make it the Standard both of *Happineß* and *Wisdom*; by concluding, That no Man can be either Happy or Wise without it: Tho' the *Scripture* tells us, That he who encreaseth in knowledge, encreaseth in Sorrow ; and daily Experience shews us, That *Folly* and *Learning* do often cohabit in the same Person. The ingenious *Montaign*, enquiring into the reason why Men of *Learning* do generally seem to be more uncouth in their Discourse as also more unfit for Busineß than other Men, saith, *I cannot conceive the true Cause hereof, unleß it be, that as Plants are Choakt by over-much Moisture, and Lamps are Stifl'd with too much Oil ; so are the Actions of the Mind overwhelm'd by over-abundance of Matter and Study : And in a diversity of things, as in a mist, the Mind*

is

is apt to lose it self. Besides, it often happens. That *Scholastick Education*, like a *Trade*, does so fix a Man in a Particular way, that he is not fit to judge of any thing that lies out of that way; Indeed, they are scarce capable of any other Thoughts; so that if a thing be never so little out of their Rode, it is altogether free from their Discovery : As I have heard of some Creatures in *Africk*, which still going a violent pace straight on and not being able to turn themselves, can never get any Prey, but what they meet just in their way. And thus we see, that *Learning* is so far from contributing to *Wisdom*, that if it be not well manag'd, it really hinders us in the pursuit of it. And a great Part of that which we call *Learning*, is like *Cobwebs*, which tho' they seem fine and Artificial, are of no Manner of use. For what is a Man the wiser for knowing the *Genitive Case* of *Jupiter*. Or whether we shou'd Write *Fælix*, or *Felix* ?

Felix ? Or what are we the Better, for knowing how many *Knots* there were in *Hercules*'s Club? Or whether *Penelope* was honeft or No? And yet as ridiculous as thefe Things are ; many of thofe Men, whom the World hath call'd *Learned*, have trifl'd away their time in thefe, and fuch like Inquiries. In a Word, it is not the knowing much, but the knowing what is ufeful, makes a Man a Wife Man. Suppofe a Man knows what is *Latin, Greek, French, Spanifh* or *Italian* for a *Horfe*, this makes the Man no more the *Wifer*, than the *Horfe* the better: Whereas if the fame Perfon had but two or three good *Receits* to cure either the *Farcy* or a *Surfeit*, this would be of real Advantage both to the *Mafter* and the *Horfe*. Thus then, if a Man have all other Points of Knowledge and *Learning*, yet if he wants that one of *Sibi Sapere*, all his other Knowledge is but Impertinence, and a Gawdy fort of Ignorance. There are indeed fome Men, who are arri-
ved

ved to a sort of *Lip-Wisdom*, as I
may so call it; who have a Knack
of talking like *Wise* Men ; by their
Discourse you would judge of 'em,
as the Ancient *Heathens* did of their
Heroes, That they were Sprung from
the *Gods* ; but if you search into
their Actions, you wou'd rather
think 'em a Kin to the *Horse* or
Mule, which have no understanding.
Odi Homines ignavos Operâ, Philoso-
phos Sententiâ, was the saying of a
great Man, *I hate Men that act like*
Fools, but speak like Philosophers.
He who *Speaks*, but does not *Act*
like a wise Man, is at best but like
a *Tinkling Cymble*, which makes
only a pleasant Noise.　Certainly,
of all Parts of *Wisdom*, the Pra-
ctick is the best.　To conclude
then, it is not a Mans cloistering
himself up in his Study, nor his
continual Poring upon Books, that
makes him a wise Man : No, this
Property is chiefly to be acquir'd by
Meditation and *Converse*.　'Tis true
(indeed) Books well manag'd afford

ford mighty Help and Affiftance:
They ftrengthen the Organ, and
enlarge the Profpect, and give a
more univerfal Infight into Things,
than can be learned from *unletter'd*
Obfervation; Whereas he who depends folely upon his own Experience, has but a few Materials to
work upon. Thefe Advantages I
fay, may be had from Books *well
manag'd* : But alafs! How Few are
there that make this ufe of their *Reading*? Or that really are one jot the
better for it? With many Men *Reading* is nothing better than a *dozing*
kind of Idlenefs, and the *Book* is a
meer *Opiate*, that makes 'em fleep
with their Eyes open. It is us'd for
no other purpofe, than as an *An-
tidote* againft *Thinking*; and they
only look upon it as the moft Cre-
ditable way for the difmiffing of
bufinefs. Such Mens *Studying* is
meerly an Artifice to reconcile the
Eafe and Voluptuoufnefs of Sloth
with the Reputation of Wifdom:
A Genteel and Wary kind of *Epi-
curifm,*

curism, that surfeits without Pain or Shame, and in which Men spend their time without Profit to themselves, or usefulness to the World. Thus then, *Thinking* is so absolutely necessary, that *Reading* signifies little, or nothing without it. *Thinking* may do without *Reading*, as appears in the first Inventers of Arts and Sciences; who were fain to *Think* out their Way to the Recesses of *Truth*; but the *Other* can never do without this. *Reading* without *Thinking* may indeed make a rich *Common-place*, but it will never enrich the Brain; it may indeed furnish a Man with great store of *Matter*, but it is still without *form* and *void*, till *Thinking*, like the *Seminal Spirit*, agitates the Dead shapeless Lump, and works it up into figure and Symmetry.

So much *Reading* then only is useful, as will excite a Mans thoughts, as will afford Hints or Sallies to the Mind, or as will furnish him with Matter for *Meditation* and *Discourse*;

which

which two Things are the two great Inſtruments of Improving our ſelves, and therefore are to preſcribe the Meaſures of our *Study* and *Reading.* Now *Reading* may very properly be compar'd to *Eating,* and *Thinking* to *Digeſting*; as therefore to one Hours Eating, we allow many hours for Digeſting; ſo to one hours *Reading,* we ſhould aſſign a Sufficient time for Meditating, and Digeſting, what we have Read. Or elſe as the one by breeding ill Humours, and obſtructing the Paſ-ſages, impairs the Health of the Body; So will the *other* be of no leſs Prejudice to the underſtanding, by occaſioning Diſeaſes to the Mind. A Man therefore may as well ex-pect to grow ſtronger by always Eating, as Wiſer by always *Read-ing.* Too much over-charges Na-ture, and as I ſaid before, turns more into *Diſeaſe* than Nouriſh-ment. 'Tis Thought and Digeſti-on which makes Books Serviceable, and gives Health and Vigour to the Mind.

Mind. Hence therefore it is, that many Men by their *Reading* so much and *Thinking* so little do instead of Improving, really impair themselves by their Studies. For by over much *Reading* they do but clog and oppress their Minds, and so digest nothing. They stuff themselves so full of other Mens Notions, that there is no Room for their own Faculties to display themselves. Whereas the Man of Thought and Meditation, moves in a larger Sphear; he does not thus *Pinion* his Fancy, but puts it upon the Wing, which seldom returns home without some Noble *Quarry*. And did Men but know, how much the Pleasure of *Thinking*, transcends all other Pleasures, they would certainly put a greater Value upon it. 'Tis an happy thing when a Mans Pleasure is also his Perfection: For most Mens Pleasures are such as debase their Nature. We commonly gratifie our lower Faculties, our Passions, and

our

our Appetites : And *thefe* do not improve, but deprefs the Mind ; and befides, they are fo grofs that the fineft Tempers are Surfeited in a little time. In fhort, there is no lafting Pleafure but *Contemplation.* All others grow flat and infipid upon frequent ufe ; and when a Man hath run through a fet of Vanities, in the Declenfion of his Age, he knows not what to do with himfelf, if he cannot *Think*. He faunters about from one dull Bufinefs to another, to wear out Time : And hath no reafon to value Life, but becaufe he's afraid of *Death*. But *Contemplation* is a continual fpring of frefh Pleafures : And nothing is comparable to the Pleafure of an Active and a Prevailing Thought ; a Thought prevailing over the Difficulty and Obfcurity of the Object, and refrefhing the Soul with new Difcoveries , and Images of Things, and thereby extending the Bounds of Apprehenfion ; and (as it were) enlarging the Terri-

H   tories

tories of Reafon. But the *Learned* Man that daily plods on in his *Reading*, and never makes ufe of this *Thinking* Faculty, by reflecting upon what he hath read, quite lofeth this *Intellectual Enjoyment* ; Nor is he fenfible of that *Suaviffima Vita*, as the Poet calls it , of *Defcending into Himfelf, and being daily fenfible of his own Improvment*: But like the Carriers Horfe, he ftill keeps the old Track ; and his *Learning* (to continue the Simile) like the Pack, is but a Burthen to the Beaft that carries it. I know, it is generally faid, That *Learning* doth conduce much both to the Difcovery, and to the Defence of *Truth*, and this indeed I cannot deny ; but then at the fame time it muft be allow'd, That only *Freedom* and *Sincerity*, are fit to be entirely trufted in that Search. For let a Man have never fo much *Learning*, yet if he be not allow'd to make a free ufe of it, but (as is the Common Cafe of moft *Clergy Men*; efpecially fuch as are
Beneficed,

Beneficed, and have Preferment ;)
is lyable to be over-aw'd by his Su-
perior for fear of Deprivation, Su-
fpenfion, or fome other Punifhment ;
I fay , in that Cafe, *Learning* gives
no Authority to his Opinion. And
for this reafon, I remember a Perfon
of very great Learning and Judgment us'd to fay, That, for his
Part, he never valued any of thofe
Books, which came out *cum Per-
miffu Superiorum*, fince their Defign
was rather to promote the Intereft
of a *Party*, than to advance *Truth*.
It is not then to be wonder'd, That
the *Clergy* in all Parts of the World,
are fo very zealous in the Afferting
and Defending the feveral Religions of their Refpective Countries ;
fince it is not only their Intereft, in
hopes of Preferment, fo to do ; but
alfo, becaufe the Civil Government
hath fo great a Check upon them,
that they durft do no other. Whereas if thefe Shackles, and Reftraints
were but taken off, *Learning* would
then(beyond all Difpute)be the beft,

and moſt proper Vehicle for *Truth:* Whatſoever then hath been ſaid a- gainſt *Learning,* thus much muſt at laſt be acknowledg'd, That when *Learning* meets with an ingenious Temper, and is join'd to a pregnan- cy of Mind, it is then of excellent uſe, and advantage : For there is no Man but will ſpeak the better, where he knows what others have ſaid upon the ſame Subject. And ſometimes the Conſciouſneſs of his inward Knowledge, gives a graceful Confidence to his outward Behavi- our. But on the other hand, if *Learning* happens to be in the poſſeſſion of a Fool, 'tis then but a Bawble, and, like *Dr. Donne's Sun Dial in the Grave,* a Trifle, and of no Uſe.

ESSAY III.

ESSAY III.

Of EDUCATION *and* CUSTOME.

WE fuck in the firſt Rudiments as we do the Common Air (*facili hauſtu*)as the Lord *Bacon* expreſſeth it , without *Diſcrimination* or *Election* ; of which indeed our tender, and unexercis'd Minds are not capable. And I con-feſs, 'tis neceſſary we ſhou'd do ſo ; nor were there any hurt in this inno-cent Eaſineſs, did not moſt Men all their Lives Worſhip the firſt Thing they ſaw in the *Morning* of their Daies, and ever after obſtinately ad-here to thoſe unexamined Recep-tions. But here lies the Miſchief, when we are *Children,* we are apt to

Be-

Believe every Thing ; and when we are grown *Men*, we seldom examine Things, but settle in their first *Im-pressions*, without giving our selves the trouble to consider, and review them. And these Prejudices, by *Cu-stom* and long Acquaintance with our Souls, get a Mighty Interest, and become irresistable to every thing that is different from those Images of Education.

> *Quô semel est imbuta recens, serva-*
> *bit odorem*
> *Testa diu.*———

Said the Heathen Poet, the first seasoning Principles and Prejudices, which we receive in our Youth, stick closely to us for a long time after. *Tully*, I remember, makes mention of a *Musician*, who being ask'd what the *Soul* was, presently repli'd, That it was *Harmony*; whereupon *Tully*, being well enough pleas'd with the Answer, makes this witty Remark, *Hic à Principiis Artis suæ*
non

non receſſit, He knew not how to leave the Principles of his own Art. So likewiſe *Plato's Scholars* had been altogether bred up in *Arithmetick,* and the knowledge *Numbers*; and therefore hence it was that afterwards when they diverted their Studies to the knowledge of *Nature,* or *Moral Philoſophy*; whereſoever they walk'd, or whatſoever they were doing, their Heads were ſtill runing upon *Numbers*. They fancied, the World was fram'd out of *Numbers*; Cities, Kingdoms, and Common-wealths, they thought ſtood by *Numbers*; *Number* with them was *Sole Principle* and *Creator* of every Thing. In a Word, it fares much with us, as it did with *Tully's Muſician,* or *Plato's Scholars, Difficulter à Principiis Atris noſtræ recedimus,* 'Tis with much Difficulty that we forſake thoſe *Principles* we have been bred up in. The wiſe Philoſopher tells us, That the *Soul* of Man is *Raſa Tabula,* like a white Sheet of Paper, out of which therefore it

muſt

muſt be more than common Art,
that can ſo clear take out the firſt
Writing, as to ſuperinduce a new
Copy fair and legible. This is the
true Reaſon, why any Perſon finds it
ſo difficult to quit thoſe Notions of
Religion, which have been eſtabliſh-
ed in his Mind from his early Infancy. There is a Marvellous A-
greement and Natural Kindneſs to
thoſe Opinions, which we ſuck in
with our Milk ; they are like *Fo-*
ſter-Brothers, to whom it has been
obſerv'd, There is as ſtrong an Inclination, as to the *Natural* ; we play
and converſe with 'em from our *Cra-*
dles and as ſoon as we can go alone,
we take 'em by the Hand ; we ſleep
with 'em in our Boſoms, and contract an inſenſible Friendſhip with
'em, a pleaſing Familiarity, which
takes off all Deformities ; we love
'em, and we like 'em, and their
very *Blackneſs* is a *Beauty*, as it is
with the *African* Nations, to whom
even that which we judge *Deformi-*
ty, appears more lovely, than the
moſt

moſt Delicate *European Beauty.* Thus it was truly ſaid of *Philo,* That every *Mans own Religion ſeem'd to him the beſt, becauſe he judgeth of it not by Reaſon, but by Affection*; like thoſe *Philoſophers* of whom *Cicero* ſpake, who approv'd of no Diſcipline but their own. Hence we find, That the beſt Account many can give of their Faith, is, That they were bred in it: And the moſt are driven to their Religion, by *Cuſtom* and *Education,* as the *Indians* are to *Baptiſm,* that is, like a drove of Cattle to the Water. Thus do we judge all Things by our Anticipations, and condemn or applaud 'em, as they differ, or agree, with our firſt Opinions. 'Tis on this Account, that almoſt every Country cenſures the *Laws,* Cuſtoms, and Doctrins of every other, as abſurd and unreaſonable, and are confirm'd in their own Follies beyond poſſibility of Conviction. In a Word, there's nothing ſo abſurd, to which *Education* cannot form our tender Youth;

it

it can turn us into Shapes more Monftrous then thofe of *Africk.* For in our *Childhood,* we are like the Melted Wax to the prepar'd Seal, capable of any Impreffion from the Documents of our Teachers. The *Half Moon* or *Crofs* are indifferent to us; and with the fame eafe can we Write on this *Rafa Tabula,* **Turk** or **Chriftian.** Hence therefore it is, that we find no Religion fo irrational, but can Boaft of its *Martyrs;* nor no Opinion fo filly and Ridiculous, but has had fome *Philofopher* or other to fupport and defend it. And becaufe there is not any thing more ftrange, than the great Diverfity of Laws, and Cuftoms in the World; I fhall not here think it impertient to tranfcribe fome of thofe, which are moft Remarkable'; as for Inftance, to account it a moft Pious and Religious Act, to kill their Parents, when they come to fuch an Age; and then to eat 'em: In one and

the

the fame Nation, Virgins go with their Privy Parts uncover'd, and Married Women carefully Cover and Conceal them : *Where* Children are excluded, and Brothers and Nephews only inherit : *Where* Chaſtity, in unmarried Women, is in no eſteem ; for ſuch may proſtitute themſelves to as many as they pleaſe, and being got with Child, may lawfully take Phyſick to make themſelves Miſcarry ; but Married Women keep themſelves Chaſt and Faithful to their Husbands. *Where* the Cuſtom was, that every Bride ſhould be proſtituted to all Comers the firſt Night, and ſhe who had entertained moſt, was moſt Honour'd : *Where* they have no mariages, and therefore Children only own their Mothers, not being able to gueſs at their Fathers : *Where* Bawdy-houſes of young men are kept for the Pleaſure of Women, as there are of Women for the Neceſſities of Men : *Where* the Servile Condition of Women is

lookt

with such Contempt, that they kill all the Native Women, and Buy Wives of their Neighbours to supply their Use: *Where* they Boil the Bodies of the **Dead**, and then dry 'em, and beat 'em to a Powder, which they mix with their Wine, and so drink it: *Where* the greatest Oath they take, is to Swear by the Name of some **Dead** Person of Reputation, laying their Hand upon his Tomb: *Where* the Ordinary way of Salutation, is, by putting a Finger down to the Earth, and then Pointing it up towards Heaven: *Where* it is the Fashion to turn their **Backs** upon him they Salute, and never look upon the Man they intend to honour: *Where*, whenever the King Spits, the greatest **Ladies** of his Court put out their **Hands** to receive it: And *Where* also the most eminent Persons about him stoop to take up his Ordure in a linnen Cloth. Thus have I Collected, and Copied out

Several

Several of thofe Cuftoms, which
to me feems the moft extravagant
and uncouth ; Whereby it plainly
appears, that there is no Opinion or Imagination fo Idle or Ridiculous , which is not eftablifht
by Laws and Cuftoms, in fome
place or other. Thus, in a word,
do we fee the mighty Power of
Cuftom and *Education* ; which is
fo great that the Rankeft Follies are counted Sacred , if Cu-
ftomary ; and the *Fafhon* is always handfom and agreeable ,
tho' never. fo uncouth, or ridiculous to an indifferent beholder. In
fhort , we are civil or uncivil ,
good or bad, foolifh or wife, or any
thing elfe according to *Cuftom* ,
which *Erafmus* calls the *Monofyllable*
Tyrant , becaufe 'tis term'd *Mos* in
Latin ; though *Pindar* Stiles her
the *Queen* and *Emprefs of the World.*
Seneca fays , that we govern our
felves not by *Reafon* but by *Cu-*
ftom ; accounting that moft honeft,
which is moft Practis'd ; and Error
serves

ferves us for a Law, when it is become Publick. *Cuftom* we know is of fo great account among *Phyficians,* that according to the great *Hippocrates* ; there is no one thing ought more to be regarded: Nay, *fays he,* whatfoever a Man is us'd to, altho' it be bad, is lefs harmful than what we are not accuftomed to, altho' in it felf it be better. And among the *Lawyers,* we fee, there is nothing more efteem'd of than *Cuftom* : Prefcription is always counted the beft Title ; and the *Common Law,* which is nothing but feveral *Cuftoms* eftablifh'd by time and experience, has always the Preference of *Statute Law,* and is efteem'd the nobler Part. Again *Cuftom* governs our very *Affections* ; and we love rather by *Cuftom,* than by *Reafon* : Hence Mothers more tenderly affect their Children with whom they commonly converfe, more than Fathers do ; and Nurfes more than fome Mothers. *Cuftom* hath likewife fuch a Power over

the

the *Imagination,* that when we are
a sleep, we often dream of thofe
Things, which our Minds moft run
upon when we are awake. And
what a mighty Influence has it
upon the outward fenfes? Which may
be perceiv'd in thofe Perfons, who
(after they have been for fome time
kept in a dark place) come into a
full and open Light ; not being
able to bear that Luminous Body,
which by its glaring feems to
dazzle and offend their Sight. And
hence it is, That thofe who live
near the *Cataracts* of *Nile,* as alfo
Thofe feveral Tradefmen whofe
Noife difpleafes us fo much, and
who dwell in Mills and Forges,
Cuftom has made it fo familiar to
them, that they are no ways dif-
turb'd with this conftant Clattering,
but reft and fleep as quietly with
the Noife, as others do without it.
Thus doth *Cuftom* fufficiently
fhew its own Force and Power,
which is Stronger than Nature, infomuch as it both alters and deftroys
Nature,

Nature, and is fo Powerful, that it cannot be deftroy'd but by it felf. To conclude then, the Power of *Cuftom* is much greater then moft Men imagine, and therefore it is, that thro' miftake we often call that the *Law of Nature*, which really is but the effect of *Cuftom*, and *Education*. That Affection, which we fay every Man Naturally bears to his own Country, whence comes it? Is it not from *Cuftom?* I know indeed, fome tells us, that this Love to our Native Soil, is by the *Inftinct* of *Nature*, as Beafts love their Dens, and Birds their Nefts : But I rather think it is from Civil Inftitution as being accuftomed to the fame Laws, the fame Ceremonies, the fame Temples, the fame Markets, and the fame Tribunals. No wonder then, that the Generality of Mankind is fo influenced by *Cuftom*, fince that *Idea* which moft Men have of *Truth* and *Reafon*, is no other, than what *Cuftom*, difpenfes to 'em. And therefore

therefore it is, that we often are fo ftrangely deluded, and impos'd upon. For *Cuftom* fays *Mountain Veils from us the true Afpect of Things. Miracles appear'd to be fo, according to our Ignorance of Nature, and not according to the Effence of Nature. The continually being accuftomed to a thing, blinds the Eye of our Judgment.* It may therefore feem ridiculous to think, there is any Common Standard of *Reafon* amongft Men ; fince that charms in one Country, which is abhorr'd in others ; and the very *Imaginary Lines* which divide *Kingdoms,* feem likewife to divide their way of *Thinking,* and to make a different *Geography* in the *Reafon* which they adore, as well as in the Earth on which they trample. Hence then it is, that all Nations are fo fond of their own *Cuftoms* : The *Greeks* and *Romans* thought all other Nations *Barbarous* in refpect of themfelves. The *Italians* call all *Oltramontani* (fuch as are on this fide the Alps) *Barbari* , as tho' none knew what *Civility* meant but they. The *Venetians* will commonly fay, when they hear a Man fpeak in a Language which they underftand not, *Mo, parlate Chriftiano*, as if no Languge were *Good* and *Chriftian like* but theirs. The *Chinefes* efteem themfelves the only Reafonable and Civiliz'd People, whence it is a Common Proverb amongft them, that the *Chinefes only fee with two Eyes , and all other Men but with one.* And thus do *We* ftill keep up the fame Humour, by judging all thofe, who differ from us in their *Cuftoms* and ufages, to be at leaft Ridiculous , if not Barbarous. Tho' (after all) the *Barbarians* are no more a Wonder to us, than we are to them; nor (it may be) with any more reafon. Thofe *Americans*, who kill their old Decrepit Parents, inftead of Believing themfelves *Parricides* , call us cruel for letting ours continue fo long in the .Miferies of old Age. And as

for

for that practice of theirs (which
to us seems so unnatural) of
eating their own Parents , they
think they do thereby give 'em
the most Noble sort of *Sepulture*,
by burying 'em in their own
Bodies, in a manner reviving 'em
again, and regenerating them by a
kind of *Transmutation*, into their
living Flesh by the means of Di-
gestion and Nourishment. And to
say the truth, there are many *Laws*
and *Customs* , which seem at the
first view to be Savage, Inhumane,
and Contrary to all Reason ; but
if they were without Passion and
soberly Consider'd ; though they
were not found to be altogether
just and good , yet at least they
might be plausibly defended by
some kind of Reason. A wise Man
therefore ought to suspend his Judgment, and not to be over forward in
Censuring and Condemning the Practices and *Customs* of other Nations ;
which sort of *Narrowness* I find many

are Subject to, and with the *Hermit*, are apt to think, the Sun shines no where, but in their *Cell*: and that all the World is Darkness but themselves. But this certainly is to measure *Truth* by a wrong Standard, and to circumscribe her by too narrow a Scantling. But to proceed : Since *Custom* hath so great a sway in all our Actions, we may well look upon it, as *another Nature*. A *rooted Habit* becomes a governing Principle, and bears almost an equal sway in us with that which is *Natural.* It is (says *Tillotson*) a kind of a *New Nature* superinduced, and even as hard to be expell'd, as some Things which are Primitively and Originally *Natural.* When we bend a Thing at first, it will endeavour to restore it self; but it may be held bent so long, till it will continue so of it self, and grow crooked; and then it may require more force and violence to reduce it to its former Straightness, than we us'd to make it crooked at first.

Mens

Mens minds are naturally of the the same *Clay* ; 𝕰𝖉𝖚𝖈𝖆𝖙𝖎𝖔𝖓 is the *Potter's* Hand, and Wheel, that forms them into Veſſels of Honour and Diſhonour. *This* of all humane Means is moſt Effectual towards the Refining and Sharpening Mens Intellects, giving them an Edge and Quickneſs ; and that the more, becauſe it takes 'em in that Age, wherein their *Faculties* are, as their *Joynts,* pliant and tractable, and ſo capable of being by Exerciſe improv'd into great Degrees both of Strength and Activity. In a Word, There is nothing tends more to the forming an Honourable and Vertuous Life, than a good 𝕰𝖉𝖚𝖈𝖆𝖙𝖎𝖔𝖓. Moſt certain it is, without *this* we are as good as loſt in our very Cradles; for whatſoever *Principles* we make choice of in our Infancy, we carry for the moſt part to our Graves ; and in a Word, 'tis the 𝕰𝖉𝖚𝖈𝖆𝖙𝖎𝖔𝖓 that makes the Man. With much Elogancy and Smartneſs, then does the Incomparable *Dryden* tell us :

I 3

" By

" By **Education** moſt Men are
" miſled ;
" So We Believe, becauſe We ſo
" were Bred :
" The *Prieſt* continues what the
" *Nurce* began ;
" And thus the *Child* impoſes on
" the *Man.*

Thus we ſee, that the leaſt falſe
Step at the firſt ſetting out, makes us
hobble and limp all the journey afterwards. Since **Education** (then)
carries ſo great force and Authority
along with it, how much does it be-
hove ſuch Parents, who have any regard to Vertue and Wiſdom, to
give their Children a Vertuous and
ſober *Education* ? Tho' indeed this
does not always prove ſucceſsful.
For *Nero,* notwithſtanding his two
excellent Tutors, *Seneca* and *Burr-*
has, receiv'd but little Improvement.
Cicero's Son to the ſtupidity of his
Nature, added Drunkenneſs, and re-
turned from *Athens,* and *Cratippus* as
arrant

arrant a Blockhead as he went.
Marcus Aurelius provided fourteen
of the moſt approv'd Maſters to
Educate *Commodus*, yet could not
rectifie his froward and barbarous
Humour. Thus, as Sir *Henry Wot-*
ton obſerves, There is in ſome Tempers ſuch a NaturalBarrenneſs, that,
like the ſands of *Arabia*, they are
never to be cultivated or improv'd.
And according to the old Proverb,
Ex quovis Ligno non fit Mercurius——
There are ſome *Crabb-Stocks* of ſuch
a Nature, that all the Ingrafting in
the World can never Correct or A-
mend. But theſe Monſters of Nature are not often to be met with:
For we uſually obſerve, That the
Culture of the *Mind*, as of the
Earth, doth deliver it from the Bar-
renneſs of its own Nature : And
that the tougheſt, and moſt unben-
ded Natures, by early and prudent
Diſcipline, may be much corrected,
and improv'd.

I 4　　ESSAY IV.

ESSAY IV.

Of the ANCIENTS: *The Respect that is due to 'em : That we shou'd not too much enslave our selves to their Opinions.*

AS we should not be so fondly conceited of our selves, and the extraordinary Abilities of the present Age, as to think every Thing that is Ancient to be obsolute ; Or, as if it must needs be with *Opinions*, as it is with *Cloaths*, where the Newest is for the most part best ; so neither should we be so superstitiously devoted to *Antiquity*, as to take every Thing for *Canonical*, which drops from the Pen of a *Father*, or was approv'd by the Consent of the *Ancients*. Antiquity is ever venerable,and
juftly

juſtly challenges Honour, and Reverence; but yet there is diffe-rence between *Reverence* and *Super-ſtition*; We may aſſent to 'em as *Ancients*, but not as *Oracles*; They may have our Minds eaſie and incli-nable, but there is no reaſon they ſhould have them Captivated and Fetter'd to their Opinions. As I will not diſtruſt all, which without manifeſt proof they deliver, where I cannot convince 'em of Error; ſo likewiſe will I ſuſpend my Belief upon probability of their Miſtakes; and where I find reaſon to *diſſent*, I will rather reſpect *Truth* than *Au-thority*. As there may be Friendſhip, ſo there may be Honour, with Di-verſity of *Opinions*; nor are we bound therefore to *Deifie* Men, becauſe we Reverence 'em. We wrong our *An-ceſtors* more by admiring than op-poſing 'em in their Errors; and our Opinion of 'em is very diſhonoura-ble, if we think they had rather have us followers of *Them*, than of *Truth*. Certainly, the greateſt Reſpect

spect we can shew the *Ancients*, is by following their Example : Which was not *Supinely* and *Superstitiously* to sit down in fond Admiration of the Learning of those who were before 'em; but to Examine the Writings, to avoid their Mistakes, and to use their Discoveries, in order to the further improvement of Knowledg. This they did, and never any Man took a greater Liberty in censuring and reproving the supposed Errors and Mistakes of the Elder Philosophers, than *Aristotle* himself ; and therefore I do not see any reason why he should be allow'd greater Priviledge, than what he himself thought good to allow to those before him. *Veritas nec Mea est nec illius, aut Ullius* , says St. *Austin*, No Man can say, *I am Infallible*; for as we are *Men*, so we are subject to *Error*. As for the *Truth* of Things, *Time* makes no Alteration ; Things are still the same they are, let the Time be *Past*, **Present**, or *to Come*. Those Things which

we .

we Reverence for *Antiquity*, what were They at their firstBirth ? Were they falfe ? Time cannot make them True : Were they True ? Time cannot make them more True. The circumftance therefore of *Time*, in refpect of *Truth* and *Error*, is meerly impertinent. For as *Antiquity* cannot priviledge an *Error*, fo *Novelty* cannot prejudice *Truth*. I know in all Ages there have been Thofe, who with a great deal of Zeal and Elegance have declaim'd againft *New Things*, fetting forth the great danger of *Alteration* and *Novelty*. But let us not be frightend with fhadows: If to be the Author of *New Things*, be a Crime ; how will the firft Civilizers of *Men*, and Makers of *Laws*, and Founders of *Governments* efcape ? Whatever now delights us in the Works of *Nature*, that excells the rudenefs of the firft Creation is *New* ; Whatever we fee in Cities, or Houfes, above the firft Wildnefs of Fields, and Meanefs of Cottages, and Nakednefs of Men, had

its

its time, when this Imputation of *Novelty* might as well have been laid to its Charge. It is not therefore an Offence to introduce *New Things*, unlefs that which is introduced prove pernicious in it felf; or cannot be brought in without the Extirpation of others, that are better. If *Novelty* fhou'd always be rejected, neither would Arts have arriv'd to that Perfection, wherein now we enjoy them, nor cou'd we ever hope for any Future Reformation. Tho' all *Truth* be in it felf *Eternal*, yet in refpect of Mens Opinions there is fcarce any fo *Ancient*, but had a Beginning, and was once counted a *Novelty*; And if for this Reafon it had been condemn'd as an *Error*, what a general darknefs and ignorance wou'd then have been in the World, in comparifon of that Light which now abounds. The great *Architect* of the World hath been obferv'd not to throw down all Gifts and Knowledge to Mankind confufedly at once, but in

a

a Regular Parſimonious Method, to diſperſe them by certain Degrees, Periods, and progreſs of Time leaving Man to make induſtrious Reſearches and Inveſtigations after *Truth* ; *he left the World to the Diſputations of Men,* as the *Wiſeſt* of Men ſays, who in the Acquiſition of Natural Truths went from the Hyſope to the Cedar ; *one Day certifieth another,* and one Age rectifieth another, and the morrow hath more Experience than the preceeding Day. Thoſe Times which we term vulgarly the *old World,* was indeed the *Touth* of it, and tho' if reſpect be had to the Particular and Perſonal Acts of Generation, and to the Relation of Father and Son, they who liv'd before us, and preceeded us, may be call'd our *Anceſtors* ; yet if you go to the Age of the World in general, and to the true length and longævity of Things, *We* are more properly the *Ancients,* and the preſent Age is the greateſt Antiquity : Hence, as the

Lord

Lord *Bacon* obferves we have generally a wrong Notion of Antiquity;
for (fays he) *to fpeak truly, Antiqui-
tas feculi, i juventus Mundi* : That
which we commonly call *Antiquity*,
is but the *Nonage* of the World :
And in this refpect, the *Younger*
Brother may be term'd more Ancient
than his *Elder*, becaufe the World
was older when he enter'd into it.
The admiring of Former Ages, was
a Vanity that poffefs'd all Times
as well as Ours; and the *Golden
Age* was never the *Prefent*. They
who went before us, have not pre-
vented us, but have opened a Door,
that we may enter into the Receffes
of *Truth* : He that comes laft hath
certainly the beft advantage in the
Inquiry. Our *Anceftors* have done
wifely and well in their Generations, but they have not done all;
much Work ftill remains behind,
and he that lives a thoufand ages
hence, fhall not have reafon to complain, That there are no hidden
Truths fit for him to Enquire after.

ter. There are more Worlds to conquer ; every day brings a newLight,
and by a wife and careful Labour,
we may improve what our Fore-Fathers fpy'd , when they peept thro'
the Crevifes. If the latter Ages
cou'd be abftracted from the mix-
ture of *Intereft*, and the Engage-
ment of their Party, they are in
many things better able to teach the
People than the *Ancients*. There
is certainly a truer, and more certain knowledge of Things, now than
formely : But that which fpoils all,
is, Men are grown a great deal more
Cunning, and few there are who
take any other Aim, than that of *Intereft*; fo that hence it is, That many times it proves fafer to rely on
the Authority of Former Ages, tho'
more ignorant than of Latter Ages,
which tho' more knowing, yet more
dangerous to follow, in refpect of
that Defign and Artifice, which now
a days Men ufe, on purpofe to
promote their own private Intereft.
In fhort, it behoves every one in the
fearch

search of *Truth*, always to preserve a Philosophical Liberty : Not to be so enslav'd to the Opinion of any Man, as to think whatever he says, to be Infallible. We must labour to find out what Things are in Themselves by our own Experience, and a thorow Examination of their Natures, not what another says of them. *Non tam Authoritas in Disputando, quàm rationis Momenta quærenda sunt,* said *Cicero* ; a Man ought not so much to regard the Person who speaks, as the Thing that is spoken. but it is the unhappy Humour of too many Men, *jurare in Verba Magistri,* servilely to tye themselves to the Authority of particular Men, and to see with other Mens Spectacles: The greatest part of the World being rather led with the Names of their Masters, and with the reverend Respect they bear their Persons or Memories, than with the Soundness and Truth of the Things they teach. Men first take up a Confidence of the Learning or Sanctity

of

of a Perſon, and then all his Notions are receiv'd implicitely, and
are ſtrictly embraced, without the
leaſt Examination : And this admiration of Mens Perſons, has in all
ages been of huge miſchief, and
very pernicious ; it has nurs'd up
private Fancies into ſolemn publick
Errors, and given an unhappy Per-
petuity to many Heterodox Opinions, which wou'd elſe have expir'd
with their firſt Defenders. Men do
not any where more eaſily err, than
where they follow a Guide, whom
they preſume they may ſafely truſt.
Belief, without Evidence of Reaſon,
muſt be only there abſolute, where
the Authority is unqueſtionable ;
And where it is impoſſible to err,
there only it is impious to diſtruſt. As for Mens Aſſertions,
Quibus poſſibile eſt ſubeſſe falſum,
what one ſaid of Friendſhip, *Sic ama*
tanquam Oſurus, love with that Wiſdom, as to remember you may be
provoked to the Contrary, is
more warrantable and advantagious
K in

in Knowledge *Sic crede tanquam Diffenfurus,* so to *Believe,* as to be ready, when cause requires to *diffent.* It is a too much Straitning of a Man's own underftanding, to enthral it unto any; and befides, there is not any thing, which hath bred more Diftempers in the Body of Learning, than Factions and Sidings; when as *Seneca* faid of *Cato,* that he would rather efteem Drunkennefs a Vertue, than *Cato* Vicious. To conclude, There is no one thing hath more ftunted the Growth of Learning, than a ftiff adhering to the Dictates of the *Ancients;* For he who makes *Plato* or *Ariftotle* the ftandard of Humane Knowledge, cannot poffibly tranfcend the Learning of *Plato,* or *Ariftotle;* the utmoft he can do, he may come up to that height, but (like *Water,*) he can never rife higher than the *Source.* I know many are of Opinion, that vaft advantages have accrued to modern Knowledge,

Knowledge, from the help and
affiftance, which the *Ancients* have
tranfmitted to us; but for my
part, I never did, or cou'd believe
any fuch thing : Nay, for ought
I know, in this refpect, we have
rather loft than gain'd by the *Ancients*; for by our Acting thus
implicitely and refigning our felves
to their Authorities, we have not
been fo careful as we ought to have
been, in preferving our Reafon in
its juft and due Liberties: And to walk
always upon Crutches, is we know
the fure way to lofe the ufe of
our Limbs. Such an abfolute Sub-
miffion (then) to the *Ancients* ,
does wonderfully cramp the parts,
and fetters the underftandings of
Men ; for fo long as they have this
narrownefs of thought, and are thus
ftreight laced, they think it a fort of Sa-
crilege to tranfcend their *Anceftors*.
Thus then for fear of out fhooting
our ForeFathers Mark, we do but Copy one after another, and fo
the Dance goes round ; nor are

we one jot the Wiser, for growing
Older.   Thofe who rely wholly
upon the help of others, and never ufe any Induftry of their own,
muft be contented to live in a conftant
Poverty. And therefore while weSu-
perftitioufly follow the Dictates of
the *Ancients*, 'tis but reafonable
to be'ieve, we break the Force,
and ftunt the Growth of our own
Genius, and by conftraining and
grafting our own Notions upon
the Opinions of others, we may
very well be thought to have gain'd
a lefs ftock of *Learning* and Knowledge, than otherwife we might
have been Mafters of, if we had
but fuffered our own Thoughts
and Fancies to have ranged more
freely, and with lefsReftraint, Thus
he who fpends all his time in
Tranflating, or Painting of *Copies*,
will never do well in making an
Original, unlefs it be in the worft
Sence.   Befides, if a Man has good
Natural Parts of his own, why
may we not believe, that too
                                much

much *Learning* may as well Suf-
focate and Stifle fuch a Man's *Invention*, as we fee too much *Wood*
heaped on the Fire, or too clofe
together, does often quite extin-
guifh and put it out. In a word,
the *Mind* as well as the *Body* re-
ceives more Strength and Vigour
from the warmth of *Exercife* than
of *Cloths* : Nay, too much of this
Foreign Heat fays Sir *William Temple*, does rather make Men faint,
and their Conftitutions more tender and weaker, than otherwife
they wou'd be ; which is agreeable
to that *Aphorifm* of *Hippocrates*,
That *all Adventitious Heat deftroys
the Natural.*

Indeed, it is wonderful to obferve, how well pleas'd fome Men
are, in propping themfelves up by
the Learning and Knowledge of
other Men ; which appears by their
many and frequent *Quotations* out
of *Authors*, and that upon every
flight occafion. No doubt the Man
valued himfelf much, and thought

the

the saying to be Learning, and an
Elegancy too, that *Men have Beards*,
and that *Women have none* ; when
he had quoted *Beza*, for it : Nor
ought he to beesteem'd less considerable for Clarkship, that cou'd tell
us, *Pax res bona est*, Saith St. *Austin*. But as silly and ridiculous
as this Humour seems to be, I find
it was once very Common among
such as affected the Reputation of
Learning; nor indeed, is it yet
quite out of use among *Pedants*,
and the Vulgar sort of *Scholars* ;
tho' all the Wiser have out grown
and do despise it ; nor is it to be
doubted, but the rest will do so
too, when once they consider, how
mean and inglorious it is, to have
our Heads and Books laden, just
as Cardinal *Campius's* Mules were
with old and useless Luggage. For
my part, I love to hear a Man speak
his own Sense; I affect not an Author who runs altogether upon
Quotations, without something of
his own too. 'Tis no great Satisfaction

faction to me, to hear only that which I may read at any time. And he who recites another Mans Words, is no more to me than a *Notary*. And therefore let thefe fort of Men value themfelves as much as they pleafe: This way of theirs, to content themfelves with other Mens Knowledge and Opinions, is certainly the Idleft and moft Superficial fort of Learning. For can any thing be eafier, than to fay, *Cicero* fays thus, or thefe are the Words of *Plato*, or *Ariftotle* ? A Mag Pie, or a Parrot wou'd fay as much as that. I remember I have read of a Rich Man at *Rome*, who at a great expence had got into his Family fome of the Ableft Men, and fuch as were the moft exquifitely skill'd in all forts of Science, whofe employment it was, always to be at his Elbow, that in cafe it fhould ever happen, there might be any difpute among his Friends upon any Subject whatfoever, that they might Sup-

K 4   ply

ply his Place, and be ready to prompt him, one with a Sentence out of *Seneca*, another with a verse of *Homer*, and the like, every one according to his *Talent*; And all this while the Block-headed *Patron* fancied his knowledge to be his own, because they being Maintained at his Charge, he thought himself justly entitled to all the Learning they possest. This is just like some of the highest Quality, who would fain have their Learning be esteem'd in proportion to those noble Libraries their Ancestors have left them; tho' at the same time (God knows)they make no more use of the Books, than the old Woman who sweeps the Library.

But to proceed; If we enquire the reason why the *Mathematicks*, and *Mechanick Arts*, have so much got the start in growth, of other Sciences: This may very well be thought, to be one considerable cause of it, that their Progress hath not been regarded by this Reverential Awe

Awe of former Difcoveries : Herein Men have acted freely without
laying any reftraint upon themfelves,
or *Embargo* upon their Intellectuals :
No Man ever thought it an Herefie
to out-limn *Apelles*, or to out-work
the *Obelisks* : It was never imputed
to *Galileus* as a Crime, that he faw
further than the *Ancients*, and that
he chofe rather to believe *his own* eyes,
than either *Ariftotle* or *Ptolomy.*
Thofe famous *Optick Glaffes*, which
are now fo Serviceable to us, are not
a jot the lefs valued, becaufe they
were not us'd by the *Ancients* ; nor
do we give the lefs credit to their In-
formations, becaufe they were *hid
from Ages.* The *Polar* vertue of the
Loadftone, was unknown to the *Ancients*, this was referv'd for latter
days ; 'and yet no Man is fo filly, to
think the vaft advantages, which accrue to Mankind by that Noble Invention, are (therefore) the lefs to
be 'efteem'd. And had the Author
of that Invention (one *Flavius Goia*, a
Neapolitane, who liv'd about three
hundred

hundre   Years ago) been of this narrow Principle, that *we are not to transcend the Bounds of the Antients* ; we must then (for want of this Discovery) have committed our selves to the Sole conduct of the *Stars* ; and as the *Ancients* did, must *We* always have been creeping near the Shoar : Then the fourth part of the Earth had been yet unknown, and *Hercules's Pillars* had still been the World's *Ne Ultra* : *Seneca's* Prophecy had been an *unfulfil'd* Prediction, and one Moiety of our Globes an Empty Hemisphere.

ESSAY V.

ESSAY V.

Whether the MEN *of this present* AGE, *are any way* Inferiour *to those of former* Ages; *either in respect of* Virtue, Learning, *or long* Life.

THAT the World doth daily decline, is an Opinion so *Universally* believ'd, that whoever goes about to defend the Contrary, presently shall be thought to maintain a Paradox. But that thing call'd *Universality,* is so slight an Evidence of Truth, That even Truth it self is asham'd of it: For what is *Universality* but a quainter Word to signifie the *Multitude*: Now humane Authority at the strongest is but weak, but the *Multitude* is the weakest

part

part of humane *Authority*;for it is the great Patron of Error, the moft eafily abus'd, and the moft hardly difabufed.   The beginning of Error may be, and generally is, from Private Perfons, but the maintainer and continuer of Error is the *Multitude.* To infer the truth of a Religion, from the Number of its Profeffors, is falfely to conclude the finenefs of the Cloth from the largenefs of the Meafure.   How vain and ridiculous then is it in the *Papifts,* who think this Argument of *Univerfality,* fo invincible a Proof of the truth of their Religion.   If *Multitude* be an Argument that Men are in the right, in vain then hath the Scripture faid, *Thou fhalt not follow a Multitude to do Evil:* For if this Argument fignifie any thing, the greater Number can never be in the wrong.   Indeed could wifhing do any good, I could wifh well. to this kind of Proof ; *Sed nunquam ita bene erit rebus humanis, ut plures fint meliores,* It will never go fo well with
Man-

Mankind , that the *Moſt* ſhall be
the *Beſt*. In ſhort , the beſt that
can be ſaid of Argument and Reaſon
drawn from *Univerſality* and *Multitude*, is this, ſuch Reaſon may
perhaps ſerve well to excuſe an *Error*, but it can never ſerve to warrant a · *Truth*. Notwithſtanding
therefore, that the opinion of the
World's conſtant Declining is ſo
firmly radicated in the minds of moſt
Men, yet this is no ſufficient reaſon, why we ſhould acquieſce in
ſuch a belief : Nor can any thing be
more Unphiloſophical, than an Im-
plicite Faith in this matter. And
therefore we ſhall now preſume to
enter upon the Subject. There are
two extreams common amongſt
Men : the one proper to young
Men, who always value themſelves
above their Predeceſſors, and like
Rehoboam, think their own little finger ſtronger than the whole Body
of their Fathers ; the other Peculiar to · old Men, who always extol
the time paſt above the preſent. *To*
ſpeak

*speak impartially, old Men, says Dr.
Brown, from whom we should expect
the greatest Example of Wisdom, do
most exceed in this point of folly ;
Commending the days of their Touth ,
which they scarce remember, at least
well understood not ; extolling those
times, which in their younger Tears
they heard their Fathers condemn, and
condemning those times, which the Gray
Heads of their Posterity shall com-
mend.* And that Old Men always
were of this temper, we may un-
derstand from *Horace*, who makes
the same Complaint of them. Now,
the reason why Old Men are so
much out of humour with the present times, I take to be this ; They
being for the most part much al-
tered from what they were in their
Youth, as to their Temper and Complexion, and being full of sad Me-
lancholly thoughts, this makes them
think the World is chang'd, whereas
in truth the Change is in themselves.
It fares with them in this Case, as
with those whose Mouth is out of
taste,

taſt, or whoſe Eyes are bloodſhot, or are troubled with the Jaundiſe, the one imagining all things bitter or four, which they taſt, and the other red or yellow which they ſee.

* *Terræq; Urbeſque recedunt.*
Virg. Æn. 3.

Themſelves being launch'd out in-to the Deep, the Trees and Houſes ſeem to go backward, whereas really the Motion is in themſelves, the Houſes and Trees ſtill ſtanding where they were. *Seneca* tells us a pleaſant Story of *Harpaſte* his Wife's Fool, who being all of a ſudden ſtruck blind, would by no means be perſwaded of her own Blindneſs, but ſtill cry'd out how dark the Room is grown. Such for the moſt part is the Caſe of Old Men, who, by reaſon of the In-firmities of their Bodies and Minds, no longer finding ſome guſt and pleaſure in the of the World, that they foun eir Youth, lay

the

the fault upon the World, instead
of imputing the same to themselves,
as they ought to do. For God
creates not Souls now with less
advantages then formerly; He is
as liberal of his Favours to us of
this Generation, as ever he was to
any before us; And Nature being
still as Wise and Powerful as hereto-
fore, and the Universal Causes the
same, their Operations must be like-
wise as perfect, and their Effects
as excellent in these days, as they
have been in any. Let not Men
therefore deceive themselves, and
think that we live in the Dregs of
Time, and what mighty advantages
the *Ancients* (as they call them) had
over us; for if *Antiquity* be to have
the preference, the advantage will
then be of our side; For *Antiquity*
consists in the old Age of the World,
not in the youth of it. 'Tis *we* are
the Fathers, and of more Authority than former Ages; because *we*
have the Advantage of more time
then they had, and Truth (we say)

is the Daughter of Time. And befides, our Minds are fo far from being impair'd, that they improve more
and more in acutenefs ; and being
of the fame Nature with thofe of
the Ancients, have, fuch an advantage beyond them, as a Pigmy hath
upon the fhoulders of a Gyant ;
from whence he beholds not only
as much, but more than his Sup-
porter doth. But fince the Queftion now to be handled, is rather of
Fact than of *Right,* the beft way
of difcuffing it, will be by compa-
ring the paft Ages with the prefent,
and that in thefe three Refpects, of
Vertue, *Learning*, and *long Life:*
1. Firft then, if we furvey the
Vices of former Times, they will
certainly appear more Barbarous
and Epidemical, than fuch as now
Reign in the World. Even to this
day, do we not efteem it an unpa-
rallell'd piece of wickednefs, That
no ftranger could enter *Sodom,* without being defiled by the Luft of the
more than bruitifh Citizens ? A Crime

fo

ſo foul, that nothing but Fire and Brimſtone could purge the ſtench of it from the World. After this, among the *Ægyptians* was that of the *Strawleſs Tax*. The *Græcians* under their wiſeſt Lawgivers approv'd of Theft, if it were committed with Art and Cunning. And Drunkenneſs was ſo uſual a Vice among them, that from thence *Pergræcari*, ſignifies *to be mad with Drink*. The *Romans* had two Rules of Drinking, which they commonly obſerv'd; the one was, to Drink down the Evening Star, and Drink up the Morning Star, *ad Diurnam ſtellam matutinam potantes*, ſaith *Plautus*; the other commonly practiſed among them, was the Drinking ſo many Healths, as there were Letters in their Miſtreſſes Name, according to that of *Martial* :

Navia ſex Cyathis, ſeptem Juſtina bibatur,
Quinque Lycas Lyde quatuor, Ida tribus.

Nor

Nor were their very Women free from this excefs : Nay, *Seneca* affures us, that even in Drinking, they fometimes out-did the Men. But to proceed. Have we any fo vain as *Xerxes*, that would think to whip the Sea into Calmnefs ? Or fo Prodigal as was *Alexander*, who, according to *Plutarch*, fpent twelve Millions of Talents upon *Hephæſtion's* Funeral ? Such a prodigious Sum, that many queftion whether at that time the Revinue of the whole World would amount to it. Or, what Prince is there in thefe days fo profufely extravagant, as *Heliogabalus*, the Emperour, who was poffefs'd rather with a Madnefs, than excefs of Prodigality ; he fill'd his Fifh-Ponds with Rofe-Water ; he fupplied his Lamps with the precious Balfam, that diftils from the Trees in *Arabia* ; he wore upon his Shoos Pearls and Precious Stones engraven by the hands of the moft skilful Artifts ; his Dining-Room was ftrew'd with Saffron, and his

Portico's .

Portico's with the dust of Gold: And he was never known to put on any Garment a second time, whether it was of the richest Silk, or woven with Gold. Then as for the *Cruelty* of former Ages, we shall find it many degrees to transcend any thing that is done in these days ; even amongst the *Jews*, who by their Religion pretended to more precisenefs, what more common amonst them, than Incest, Fratricide, Parricide, Sawing Men to Death, and the most Barbarous forts of Cruelties, oftentimes commited only for the diversion, and entertainment of Princes ? What Action did ever carry in it fo much of Inhumanity, as that of the thirty *Athenian Tyrants*, who caused the Daughters of some of the Slain Citizens to dance, in the Blood of their own Parents, who had newly been Murder'd by them? *Lucius Florus* tells us, that the *German* Women, in their Wars with the *Romans*, would very commonly take their Naked Sprawling

Infants,

Infants, and throw them in the face of thofe they fought 'with; thinking that fo Inhuman a Spectacle might daunt the *Roman* Courage. Was there ever fince then, any thing like the *Ten Perfecutions* ? What but *Nero's Luxury*, could ever compare with *Nero's Cruelty* ? And yet *Domitian*, in one particular, out-went him ; for he took delight in feeing thofe Torments executed , which *Nero* but commanded. What fhall I now fay of *Servius Galba*, who, when he was in *Spain*, having affembled together the Inhabitants of three Cities, to confult (as he pretended) about their common fafety, at one ftroke cut off feven thoufand of them, among whom were the very Flower of their Youth ? I might alfo tell you of *Licinius Lucullus*, who, contrary to exprefs Articles, put to the Sword twenty thoufand of the *Caucæi*, after they had furrender'd: And of *Octavianus Auguftus*, who, after the taking of *Perufia*, at one Sacrifice offer'd up the lives of three

L 3   hundred

hundred of the Principal Citizens
at the Altar of his Uncle *Julius*: And
of *Antoninus Caracalla*, who being
incensed against the Citizens of
Alexandria upon the account of some
jests they had made of him, entred
into the City in a peaceable manner,
and summoning before him all the
Youth, he surrounded them with
his Souldiers, who, upon the Sig-
nal given, fell immediately upon
them, and slew every Mothers Son
of them; and afterwards using the
like Cruelty upon the rest of the
Inhabitants, he utterly destroy'd that
most Spacious, and Populous City
of *Alexandria*. Thus could I easily
give many more instances, to shew
the wickedness of former Ages, not
only in respect of their Barbarous
Cruelties, but of their other Vices;
but I forbear this, since I very well
know, that the Character of those
Times cannot be better described,
than is already by the *Apostles*, in
their several *Epistles*: For what a
Monstrous Catalogue of Sins do
we

we meet with in the firſt Chapter to the *Romans* ; Sins of ſo deep a dye, and of ſo horrid a nature, and ſuch an Inventory of all ſorts of wickedneſs that one might very well imagine the Apoſtle had been rather deſcribing ſome *Viſion of Hell*, than the *Seat of the* Roman *Empire.* To conclude then this Point, let us not imagine that ever any Age was, or will be, free from Vice and Enormities ; while Humane Nature continues, there will be Frailties : *Vitia erunt donec Homines erunt* , ſaith *Tacitus*, Vice hath always had a being in the World, and will continue as long as Men are upon Earth. How unreaſonable is it, to think that *Man* can be better out of *Paradiſe* , than he was in it ? *Nemo ſine Crimine*, The beſt of Men have their Imperfections. We are no Angels upon Earth, but are always tranſported with ſome Infirmity or other ; and 'twill be ſo while theſe frail, fluxible humours reign within us. This as I conceive is that *Black Bean*,

L 4   which

which the *Turkiſh Alchoran* ſpeaks
of, when they feign, That *Mɪho-*
met being aſleep among the Mountains of the Moon, two Angels
deſcended, and ripping open his
Breaſt, they took his Heart, and
waſh'd it in Snow, and afterwards
pull'd out a *Black Bean*, which was
the portion of the Devil, and ſo
replaced the Heart. All things here
below run in a kind of Circle; And
as in Arts and Sciences, ſo likewiſe
in the Manners of Men there is
a Viciſſitude and Revolution. Virtue and Vice have no ſetled Habitation; every Climate hath had its
turn: Sometimes one Country carries it for Vertue and Learning, and
ſometimes another. *Athens*, which
was formerly the only place for
Learning and Civility, is now quite
over-run with Barbariſm and Ignorance. Every Nation hath its *Achme*,
or higheſt pitch of Elevation; And
when once the ſpoke of the Wheel
is uppermoſt, it ſoon whurries to the
bottom. As a Kingdom riſes in Empire,

pire, fo it enlarges both in Vertue and Vice ; and when it declines, fo the Declenfion of thefe is proportionable. And though as to particular Kingdoms, one time may be either better or worfe than another ; yet take the World in Grofs, and lump it together, we fhall find that Humane Nature is much at the fame Standard, as it was formerly ; And as we commonly obferve of the Sea, That as it gets in one place, it lofes in another ; fo every Age may make the fame Obfervation of the Vertues and Vices of Mankind.

2. The next thing to be confider'd, is, whether *former* Ages excell'd the *Prefent* in refpect of Learning. Of all the Ancients there were none more efteem'd for Learning than the *Ægyptians* : The old *Ægyptian* Learning was fo Famous, that the Spirit of God, fets forth the Eminency of *Mofes's* Knowledge by his skill in it, and the Matchleffnefs of *Solmon's* Wifdom by its exceeding it ; And therefore we may very well conclude, that the *Ægyptian*

tian Learning in those days, was
conversant about more generous and
more useful Notices, than afterwards; such as *Geometry, Astronomy,
Policy, Phisick,* and other such like
Arts, which either were perfective
of their Rational Faculties, or did
Minister to the Uses and Necessities
of Nature : As is generally reported by all Ancient Historians.
But had the Primitive Learning of
Ægypt been the same it was in latter
Ages, it had been as great a dispa-
ragement to *Moses,* as 'tis now justly
reputed a Commendation, That he
was accomplished in all the *Ægyptian* Learning, and had amounted
only to this, That he was a vain
trifling, Superstitious Fellow. And
what the *Ægyptian* Priest objected
to the *Greeks, That they were always Children,* might be more truly
applied to themselves, if it be the
property of Children to value trifles.
What Childish Fooleries their *Hieroglyphicks* were , Learned Men
now prove from the lost labour, and
fruitless

fruitlefs Induftry of *Kircher's Oedi-
pus Ægyptiacus.* Certainly, if they
had defign'd to abufe and debauch
this humour, they could fcarce have
contriv'd more fond and extravagant Emblems; and indeed their
Courfenefs, and Unlikenefs to the
things they fhould refemble, fufficiently difcover them to have been
but the rude Eſſays of a Barbarous
and Undifciplin'd *Fancy.* *Thefe Hieroglyphicks,* fays the Learned Bifhop *Wilkins, feem to be but a flight,
imperfect Invention, fuitable to thofe
firft and ruder Ages; much of the
fame Nature with that* Mexican *way
of Writing by Picture, which was a
meer fhift they were put to, for want
of the Knowledge of Letters. And it
feems to me queftionable,* fays the
fame Author, *whether the Ægyptians
did not at firft ufe their* Hieroglyphicks *upon the fame account, namely,
for want of Letters.* The Lord
Herbert of *Cherbury,* fpeaking of thefe
Hieroglyphicks, fays, they were
firft invented by *Priefts,* rather to
hide

le their Opinions, or perchance their Ignorance, than to inftruct others. But for all this, it is fcarce credible what a mighty noife this *Hieroglyphick* way of Philofophizing hath made, though there is fo little of fubftance in it, and how exceedingly it took in the Infancy of the World; as it is the property of Children, to be taken more with fenfible Forms, Shadows, or Pictures, which pleafe the Fancy, than with folid Reafon. Indeed, to a Man that confiders it, nothing could ever feem more prepofterous to the defign of Learning, than thefe *Hieroglyphicks,* or Myftical Reprefentations, which were unavoidably clogg'd with two Inconveniencies, very unfuitable to the propagation of *Knowledge,* which were *Obfcurity* and *Ambiguity* : For it not only coft them a great deal of Time to gather up fuch *Symbolical* Things, which might reprefent their Conceptions ; but when they had pitc'd upon them, they were lyable to a great variety of *Inter-*

pretations,

pretations, as is evident in all thofe remainders of them, preferved by the Induftry of fome Ancient Wriers. I cannot therefore imagin any rational Man could think that Study worth his pains, which at the higheft can amount but to a *Conjecture;* and when it is come to that with a great deal of pains, it is nothing but fome ordinary and trivial Obfervation. *Certainly* (faith the Learned *Stillingfleet*) *this kind of Learning deferves the higheft form among the D I F F I C I L E S NU-G Æ, and all thefe* Hieroglyphicks *put together, will make but one good one, and that fhould be for* LABOUR LOST. I might here (if it were not too great a Digreffion) fhew how very Pernicious the ufe of thefe *Hieroglyphicks* were to the Vulgar, who feeing the *Attributes* of *God* reprefented under the fhapes of *Animals* and *Plants,* took occafion to adore thofe Corporeal Things, and fo became the moft Superftitious of all Nations, going fo far as to deifie
Garlick

Garlick, Onions, Rats, and *Toads.*
But to proceed: The truth of it is,
the *Ægyptians* feem to have had only Knowledge enough, to know that
their Neighbours had none at all,
and cunning enough to pretend an
infpection into ftrange and abftrufe
Myfteries; knowing that others by
reafon of their Ignorance could not
controul them, and by reafon of
their Credulity would be very apt
to credit them; and thence they
continually abus'd the Credulous
Grecians with Tales and Fables. The
Learned *Stillingfleet* tells us, There
wanted not grounds of Sufpicion, that
the old *Ægyptian* Learning was not
of that Elevation, which the prefent diftance of our Age makes us
apt to think it was. And the
Learned *Conringius,* in his Book *de
Hermeticâ Medicinâ,* hath endeavour'd to fhew the great defects there
were in it. *Nor can it, I think, be deni-
ed,* faith Stillingfleet, *but according to
the reports we have now concerning the
old* Ægyptian *Learning, fome parts*
of

of it were *frivolous*, others *obscure*, a
great deal *Magical*, and the rest *short*
of *what Improvement*, which the ac-
cession of the parts and industry of
after *Ages* gave unto it. It were
easie to shew, how much even those
parts of Learning, wherein the Æ-
gyptians and the other *Ancients* did
most excel, have been improved in
these latter Ages ; but this Task
having been performed by abler
Pens, I shall only touch upon three
Things, so very useful to Mankind,
viz. Anatomy, Geography, and *Navigation* ; to shew what a mighty
improvement they have received in
this last Age. First then, as for *A-
natomy* ; This Art was doubtless in
very little use among the Ancients.
I know indeed, there are some who
tell us, that the *Ægyptians* were
very accurate in the knowledge of
Anatomy ; but when I consider how
excessively Curious and Ceremoni-
ous, or rather Superstitious they
were in preserving their Bodies en-
tire and unputrified, I cannot but
conceive

conceive their opening them was rather for the *Embowelling*, than the *Anatomizing* of them. As for the *Grecians*, this Art could not well be in practice among them, because their usualCustom was to Burn their dead Bodies, as we find it attested by *Homer, Herodotus, Thucydides*, and *Plutarch*; and besides, had *Anatomy* been in use among the *Grecians*, there is no dispute but the works of *Hipocrates*, yet extant, would have discovered it, which we do not find in any place they do : Nay, so far from that, that *Hipocrates* himself going one time to visit *Democritus*, he happen'd to find him busie in Dissecting several Beasts, who asking him what he meant by his being so employ'd, *Democritus* (by way of Apology) makes him this reply, *Hæc Animalia quæ vides propterea seco, non Dei opera perosus, sed fellis bilisque naturam disquirens.* Now, if he apprehended that the Dissecting of *Beasts* might be lookt upon as an *hating of Gods works*, he might

might much more have feared that censure, had he cut up the Bodies of *Men.* Nor does it appear by a- ny thing extant in the Writings of *Galen,*that that other *Father of Phi- ficians,* ever made any *Anatomy* of Humane Bodies. Nor was this Art practifed among the *Romans,* nor in- deed could it be; forafmuch as they held it unlawful, *Afpicere humana exta,* (as *Pliny* in his Preface to his 28 Book tells us) to look up- on the Entrals of Mens Bodies, And *Dion* in his 55*th* Book fays, That it was allowed to *Tiberius* to touch the Body of *Auguftus, Quod nefas alias erat,* which otherwife had been unlawful. And that the *Pri- mitive Chriftians* favour'd not the Practice of *Anatomy,* will plainly appear from*Tertullian,*who in the 4*th* Chapter of his Book *de Anima,*fpeak- ing of one *Herophilus,* doubts whe- ther to call him *Medicum* or *Lanium,* a *Phyfician* or a *Butcher, Qui Ho- minem odiit, ut noffet,* faith he, who hated Man, that he might know him : And St. *Auguftine* in his

M   2 *3 d*

22*d* Book *de Civ. Dei. Cap.* 24. runs much upon the same strain. And among others we find Pope *Boniface* the 8*th* such a profes'd Enemy to this art of diffecting Humane Bodies, that he threatens immediately his *Thunderbolt* of *Excommunication* to all such as should do any thing of this nature.　Thus we see how very shie and unacquainted the *Ancients* were with this most excellent Art, which certainly is one of the most useful in humane Life, as tending most to the Evifcerating, and difclofing the fecrets of Nature. But now in thefe latter Ages, we have taken off this thick Veil of Superftition, and there is fcarce any Man, who has not a defire to know, *How curiously and wonderfully he is made.*　Hence then *Anatomy* hath of late been a *free* and *general Practice* ; and particularly in this Age it hath receiv'd wonderful Improvements. For proof whereof I need not take much pains, fince there is. no Man that hath the leaft infight into Phyfick, but

but khows how much the Learned
Dr. *Harvey* in that excellent Treatife of his, *De Generatione Anima-
lium,*hath tranfcended all that went
before him, in that full and fatis-
factory account he there prefents
the World with, concerning the
Conftitution, Structure, and Nutrition of Humane Bodies : What a
mighty name hath he juftly got in
the *Orbis Literarius,* by that wonderful and furprizing difcovery of
the *Circulation of the Blood* ; a Doctrine foUniverfally embraced,and fo
unqueftionably true, that a Phyfician would be thought aHeretick *pri-
mæ Claffis,* who fhould in the leaft
difpute it? How much is the whole
Colledge of Phyficians indebted to
the memory of the Famous Dr. *Glif-
fon,* for giving them a more true and
perfect account of theNature of San-
guification, Bilification, Separation
of Urine, and other Humours from
the Mafs of Blood, than ever the
World was formerly acquainted
with? And does not the Incompara-

M 2   ble

ble Dr. Willis deserve to be reckon'd among the Benefactors of Mankind, for those great Discoveries he hath made of Nutrition, Generation, and Separation of the *Succus Nervosus,* and Animal Spirits, with their præternatural affections? How glimmering a light, and how imperfect a notion had the Ancients of the nature of the *Saliva,* and other Juices that are convey'd into the Mouth, together with their Passages; until our Learned and Famous Country-Man, Dr. *Wharton,* and of late the Learned *Steno* so happily disclos'd those Secrets of Nature? Did any of the Ancients ever imagine, that the Lungs consisted only of Vessels and Bladders? That the Liver, Spleen, and Reins were *Conglomerate Glandules;* and yet that these are so, that expert Anatomist, and great Naturalist, *Malphighius,* hath informed the World? Which of the Ancients ever dreamt, That the Testicles of the Male should be nothing but a *Conglomeration of Vessels;*

Veſſels ; and the Female Teſticles , *Ovaries* ; was not this Diſcovery alſo an honour reſerv'd for the preſent Age, and to the Induſtrious and Learned *De Graef* are the thanks due? Who among the *Ancients* ever rightly inform'd us as to the Operation of *Cathartick* Medicines in Humane Bodies : Or as to the Reaſon of the different Colours, of the *Excrements*, that are obſerv'd to be evacuated by them, until that great *Anatomical* Light, *Sir George Ent*, imparted it to the World ? Which was it of the *Ancients*, that ever had a true notion how the *Chyle* was convey'd into the Maſs of Blood ? We very well know, they told us it diſcharg'd it ſelf through the *Meſeraick* Veins into the Liver ; but as to its true Paſſage into the Blood, they were as little able to give an account of that, as they were to demonſtrate the Commixture of the Air therewith ; and yet they had the confidence to teach it in their Schools as an *Ens Rationis* , though they

M 3 they

they had never made any Proof, or
Experiment for the truth of this Affertion.   In what a high Meafure
then did that great Anatomift Dr. *Lo-*
wer, oblige the World, by his great
Induftry and indefatigable Pains, who
in that rare and admirable Tract of
his, *De Corde*, hath not only more
punctually fhew'd the true paffage
of the *Chyle* through its Lacteals, Re-
ceptacle, and Chyliferous ducts, than
formerly, but hath plainly demonftrated that it is impoffible there can
be any other, by which it fhould
have its difcharge into the Mafs of
Blood ? Nor are his Arguments lefs
nervous and cogent, for proving the
Commixture of the nitrous Particles
of the Air with the Mafs of Blood.
Thus have I given you an account
of feveral of the moft confiderable
Improvements made in this prefent
Age, in that part of Phyfick relating to *Anatomy* ; all which ingenious and excellent Inventions, are of
great ufe, as affording us better Hy-
'pothefes in Phyfick, and by Confequence

fequence tending to a better and more effectual way of Curing Difeafes.

The next thing that falls under our Confideration, is, to fhew how much *Geography* hath lately been Improv'd. The *Ancients* were fo very defective in this Art or Science, that the Learned *Varenius* tells us, That the moft General and Neceffary Things belonging threunto, were then unknown; as the Flux and Reflux of the Sea; the Habitablenefs of the Torrid Zone; the Polar Property of the *Magnet*; the diverfity of Winds, the true dimenfion of the Earth: Nor had they any true Defcriptions of remote Countries, concerning which both the *Greeks* and *Romans* had very fabulous Relations; they knew not that the Earth was encompaffed by the Sea, and might be failed round; They were totally ignorant of *America,* and both the *North* and *South* parts of this Hemifphere; yea, and underftood very little of the

M 4 'remoter

remoter parts of their own *Afia*;
That part of the *Indies* that lies on
the other fide of the River *Ganges*,
was in a manner a *Terra Incognita* to
them; they knew little or nothing
of the vaft Kingdom of *China*, nothing of *Japan*, or the numerousO-
riental Iflands, and thefe made a
great, if not the beft part of *Afia*.
But that which to me feem'd ftranger, or more remarkable, is, That
neither *Thucydides* nor *Herodotus*,
nor any other *Greek* Author Cotem-
porary with them, have fo much as
mention'd the *Romans*, though then
growing up to a dreadful Power,
and being both *Europeans*. *Budæus*
in his 4*th* Book *De Affe*, tells us,
That the *Grecians* were fo utterly
ignorant of the *Spaniards*, that *E-
phorus*, one of their moft accurate
Geographers, took *Spain*, which he
calls *Iberia*, to be a City. It was
in former times counted fo dangerous a thing to believe the *Antipodes*, that *Boniface*, Arch-bifhop of
Mentz, by chance feeing a Treatife
written

written by *Virgilius*, Bifhop of *Saltz-burg*, touching the *Antipodes*, think-ing that fome Damnable pernicious Doctrine might be couched under that ftrange Name, complain'd firft to the Duke of *Bohemia*, and af-terwards to Pope *Zachary, Anno.* 745. By whom the poor Bifhop (whofe great misfortune was to be Learned in fuch a blockifh Age)was condemn'd as a *Heretick.* Nay, even St. *Auftin, Lactantius,* and fome other of the Ancient Writers, do by no means allow of the *Antipodes*, but look upon it to be a ridiculous, in-credible ftory; and Venerable *Bede* is much of the fame Opinion. The Learned *Fracaftorius* faith, That our Anceftors knew little *Weftward* be-yond the *Fortunate Iflands*, and *Eaft-ward* as little beyond *Catygara*, now call'd *Canton*, the Richeft City in *China*; So that (as that Learned Au-thor informs us) of the whole Ha-bitable World, fcarce one half was known to the *Ancients.* Now, by the account I have here given, it
plainly

plainly appears, how grosly ignorant the *Ancients* were in the knowledge of *Geography*, as also what a
vast Improvement it hath received
in these latter Days: For our Navigation is far greater, our Commerce is more general, our Charts
more exact, our Globes more accurate, our Travels more remote, our
Reports more intelligent and sincere;
and consequently, our *Geography* far more perfect, than it was in
the Elder Times of *Polybius* and
Possidonius; yea, than in those of
Ptolomy,*Strabo*,and *Pomponius Mela*,
who liv'd among the *Cæsars*. And
if this Art was so very defective
in the flourishing times of the *Roman*
Empire, there is no dispute but it
was much more so, in the days of
Aristotle and the *Græcians*: And
therefore no wonder the *Macedonian
Touth* was no better instructed, than
to believe he had Conquer'd the
whole World : When (God knows)
there were Nations enough, both
before him and behind him, to have
swallow'd

fwallow'd up the *Young Commander*, and his *Triumphant Armies*, at a Morfel. But as great an Improvement as hath in thefe latter Ages been made in the knowledge of *Geography*, we have yet reafon to believe, That our Difcoveries may ftill be inlarged to further Countries, a good proof whereof it is, That fo many fpacious Shores, and Mountains, and Promontories appear to our *Southern* and *Northern* Sailors ; of which we have yet no account, but only fuch as could be taken by a remote Profpect at Sea: From whence, and from the Figure of the Earth, it may be concluded, That almoft as much fpace of Ground, remains in the Dark, as was fully known in the Times of the *Affyrian* or *Perfian* Monarchy. So that without affuming any vain *Prophetick* Spirit we may foretel, That the Difcovery of another *New World* is ftill behind. To accomplifh this, there is only wanting the Invention of *Longitude*. This if it fhall be

once

once accomplifh'd, will make well nigh as much alteration in the World, as the Invention of the *Needle* did before.   And then our *Posterity* may out-go us, as much as we can travel further than the *Ancients*; whofe *Demi-Gods*, and *Heroes* did efteem it one of their chief Exploits, to make a journey as far as the *Pillars* of *Hercules*.   Whofoever fhall think this a defperate Bufinefs, can only ufe the fame Arguments, wherewith *Columbus* was at firft made ridiculous : If he had been difcourag'd by the Raillery of his Adverfaries, by the judgment of moft *Aftronomers* of his Time, and even by the Intreaties of his own Companions, but three days before he had a Sight of Land, we had loft the knowledge of half the World at once.

I am now come to the laft *Parallel,* and that is, to fhew what vaft Improvements the Art of Navigation hath received in thefe laft Ages.   *Cardan,* a great fearcher into the Curiofities of Nature, tells us, That

That among other late Noble Inventions, that of the *Mariners Compaſs*
is the moſt worthy of Admiration,
as being of the greateſt Uſe and Convenience to Mankind. By the help
hereof, we are now able to find out
a way through the *vaſt Ocean,* in
the greateſt Storms and darkeſt
Nights, where is neither Path to
follow, nor Inhabitant or Paſſenger
to enquire ; It points out the way
to the skillful Mariner, when all other helps fail him, and that with
greater certainty than the wit of
Man can poſſibly do. By means
hereof, are the Commodities of all
Countries diſcover'd, Trade, Traffick, and Humane Society maintain'd, their ſeveral Forms of Government and Religion obſerv'd, and
the whole World made as it were
one *Common-Wealth,* and the moſt
diſtant Nations, *Fellow Citizens* of
the ſame *Body Politick.* But the beſt
way to make us rightly value the
bleſſing of this Invention, is, by
conſidering the many Shifts and Inconveniences

conveniences the Ancients were put to, for want of it. We may easily Imagine, how Inconvenient the Ancients found it to sail by the guidance of the Stars : For in dark Cloudy weather, when their *Pleiades*, *Helice*, and *Cynosura* were not to be seen, the *Pilot* was always at a loss for his Guide, and knew not how to steer his Ship, but lay expos'd to the casual conduct both of Winds and Tides. And for this reason, the Ancients seldom or never durst venture into the main Ocean, but were fain to go creeping along by the Shoar side: And no more than this (as we have reason to believe) did the *Phœnicans* and *Carthaginians*, the *Tyrians* and *Sydonians*; who though renowned in History for great *Navigators*, yet by the most Learned are thought to have perform'd their Voyages only by *Coasting*, and not by *Crossing* the Ocean. Hence therefore it was, That the Commerce and Communications of those days were very inconsiderable ; Their famed

famed Travels in Comparison were nothing : And that renowned ten years Voyage of *Ulysses* (so highly celebrated by the Poets of Old) was much short of what many of our Merchants do now every Year perform. Thus you see how very defective the Ancients were in this Art of Navigation, the Benefits and Advantages whereof are so very Considerable, That the Wealth and Strength of a Nation are really to be computed in Proportion to their flourishing herein. It was long since a wise and true Observation of *Cicero, Qui Mare tenet, eum necesse est* RERUM *potiri,* He that commands the Sea, must necessarily enjoy all things. There is not any thing can be a greater Demonstration of the Flourishing of a Nation, than when its Genius lies towards *Naval* Affairs, and when by its Industry it is arriv'd to a Soveraignty of the *Seas*; This is the true Characteristical mark of the greatness of Empire : For whoever is Master of the Ocean does

does *ipso facto* command the Trade of the World, and whoever hath the Command of that, hath the Abfolute difpofal of the Riches of the World, and that Money is that which governs Mankind, is a Demonftration as clear as any in *Euclide*. Thus without the leaft ftraining of the Argument, we fee it naturally follows, that nothing is more vain or ridiculous, than for a Prince, or State, to pretend to an uncontrolable Greatnefs, that hath not firft laid their Foundation in the Deep. And who can be a better inftance of this than that Great Emperour *Charles* the *Fifth*, whofe carelefnefs in his *Naval* concerns not only broke his own Defign as to the *Univerfal Monarchy*, but likewife terminated in the ruine of his *Succeffor* ? And this overfight or neglect (though too late) that great Prince was fenfible of, when he fo ftrictly gave it in Charge to his Son *Philip*, That if either he would be happy at Home, or Confiderable Abroad, he

fhould

should take care to make himself
Great at Sea. By his Example then,
let no Prince, who aspires to be
great, slight or neglect this *Watry
Element* ; since 'tis but a *jest* in Politicks, and an *Utopian* Fancy, to
think to arrive at the utmost height
of Empire, without *Fleets* and *Ar-
mada's* : And that Prince who thinks
to give Law to Mankind, must be
sure in the first place to make the
Sea his Friend. This (without a
Figure) is to build upon a Rock,
whoseFoundation will stand firm and
sure. And therefore that Spirit of
Lazineſs, which makes the Spainard
ſo much slight this Rule, is that,
which (in ſpight of the Wealth of
the Weſt *Indies*) keeps him ſo poor
and beggarly : And while he ſits
idle at home, ſwelling with his own
Pride, the *Engliſh* and *Dutch* (by
their Induſtry) grow Rich by his
Spoils, and with his Treaſure of
the *Weſt Indies*, do they carry on
the Trade of the *Eaſt*. Thus you ſee,
the improving of Trade and Com-

N   merce

merce, is no such slight matter ;
Nor is it to be wonder'd, that this
does so often prove the Ball of Contention ; for men may well be allowed to be zealous, when their interest is so nearly concern'd ; and
this that wise and Glorious Princess,
Queen Elizabeth, very well knew,
when she so narrowly ey'd and observ'd the *Dutch,* whom she was always jealous of, left they should
grow too great in Navigation, and
so by that means might prove our
Competitors both by Sea and Land.
Since then Commerce and Navigation bring such mighty advantages
to a Nation, 'tis no wonder, I say,
that the greatest and wisest States,
and Governments, have been so very
follicitous for the improving it. *Trade*
is the very Life and Soul of the
Universe, which, like the *Vital* Blood
in the Body, Circulates to the
Health, and well-being of the whole,
and when by the failure of Industry,
there is a stop put to *Commerce,* it
often proves as fatal to the *Body Po-*
litick,

litick, as the ftagnating of the Blood
does to the *Natural Body.* What
were the World but a rude and dull
Indigefted Lump, a noifome and pe-
ftilential Mafs, did not *Commerce,*
like the *Sun,* by its *Univerfal* Rays,
exhale all its malignant and noxious
Vapours, and by a continual Motion and Tranfaction, render it whole-
fome and profitable? What would
become of the *Bufie Soul* of Man, had
fhe not found out variety of Imploy-
ment for its Exercife ? And therefore *Nature* wifely did forefee the
many and great Inconveniencies of
Idlenefs, how that it would Convert the World into another *Chaos,*
making the *Earth* but as one dull and
ufelefs *Mafs,* when fhe hid her Ra-
rities and Treafures in the fecret Bo-
wels thereof, and buried them in the
Watry Deep, and lodg'd them at fo
vaft and remote a diftance, that fo
their *Worth* and *Value* might be a
Spur to *Labour* and *Induftry* to fetch
them thence. Nay, God himfelf is
particularly call'd *the God of the Ifles,*

as looking on them, by Virtue of
their skill in *Navigation*, to be the
best *Factors* for the *Common Good*; and
as a Blessing upon their Industry,
we find most *Isles* and Maritime
places exceed all In-land Cities and
Countries in Riches, and Variety of
Plenty. We see then, 'tis not the
vastness of Territory, but the Convenience of Situation; nor the Multitude of Men, but their Address
and Industry, which improve a Nation. Now, since we have hither-
to discours'd of Trade in general,
and the several Advantages that accrue from thence; possibly the Reader may not think it altogether impertinent, if we entertain him with
an Account of the Original of *Trade*,
and shew how, and by what steps
and Methods *Commerce* hath advanced it self amongst Mankind. The
first of all Humane Race, when
they were dispers'd into several
Lands, were at first sustain'd by the
Fruits of the *Earth*, which fell to
their share. These at first they che-
rished,

iished, and us'd, not by any *Rules* of *Art*, but by that *Natural Sagacity*, which teaches all Men to endeavour their own Prefervation. And that they might peaceably enjoy thefe, they thought the beft Courfe they could take, was to Affociate themfelves into Families, and to enter into little Leagues, and thus begun *Civil Government*. But finding that no Place was fo fruitful as to produce all Things neceffary for Humane Life ; this put them upon a Neceffity, either of taking by force what their Neighbours poffefsed, or elfe of Exchanging the feveral Produ&ions of their refpe&ive Soils. This then was the way and Method of *Trading*, in the firft Ages of Mankind ; when one had eaten or fpent what was his own, he repair'd to his Neighbour for more, at the fame time accommodating him with fome other Thing whereof he ftood in need, by way of Exchange, the refpe&ive value of the Things being limited according to

their

their eftimation of their goodnefs
and fcarcity, in the firft place; and
then of their Beauty or Comelinefs.
And becaufe Oxen and Sheep afFor-
ded them the moft Commodities,
as their skins for Clothing, and
their Milk and Flefh for Food,
befides other ufes to which they
were ferviceable, they made all
their Traffick with *Cattle*, in
which their whole wealth confi-
fted. But becaufe 'twas too trouble-
fome a thing for Man to drive always a Flock of Sheep before him,
or lead a Cow by the Horn, for
making of payment; the Induftry
of Men encreafing, they caft their
Eyes upon that which was in the
next degree of moft ufe to them, and
moft durable; and finding that nothing was of more general ufe than
Iron and *Copper*, and efpecially that
the latter was the faireft, and eafi-
eft to be melted, and caft into Ket-
tles and other Domeftick Utenfils,
they made choice thereof, mutually
giving and receiving it, by Weight,
for

for other things they needed, and divided it by *Pounds*, which word ftill remains amongft us, to fignifie Twenty Shillings, which is very near the juft value that a Pound of *Copper* had in thofe days. And to fave the Labour of weighing this *Pound*, and the parts of it, they ftamp'd upon one fide the Figure of a *Ship*, with the weight and value; and on the other fide the Picture of one of thofe *Beafts*, which are defign'd by the word *Pecus*, whence *Money* came to be call'd *Pecunia*. Afterwards the *Arms* of the *Prince* were fubftituted inftead of the *Ship*, and *Conftantine* put a *Crofs* in the place of the *Beaft*. Now becaufe, in the old *Gaulifh* Language, a *Ship* was call'd *Pile* (whence the Word *Pilote* remains to this day) the fide of the *Coin* on which the *Ship* was is ftill call'd *Pile*, and the other *Crofs*, how different ftamps foever have fucceeded fince. This was the *firft Original* of *Trade*, which from a narrow Commerce between the Hills, the Vallies, the Woods, the Plains, and the Rivers,

N 4   that

that border'd one upon another, is since extended to the whole Compass of the Earth. And now 'tis high time to dismiss this Subject of *Navigation* and *Trade*; and therefore having already demonstrated, how much thePresentAge hath transcended Former Ages in those three partsofLearning,*viz.Anatomy,Geography*, and *Navigation*, I now proceed.

If from the first Ages of the World we turn our eyes to latter Times, I mean, to the Times of *Popish* Darkness, we shall Comparatively find that great is the light we now enjoy. Ignorance (we know) is the Mother of their Devotion and the very Essence of *Popery*, therefore no wonder that before the Reformation Learning was at so low an Ebb. That the *Clergy* had scarce Knowledge enough, to read the Liturgy, and the Laity no more Clarkship that to save them from Hanging. King *Alfred* in his Preface upon the *Pastorals* of St. *Gregory* (which he translated into *English*) says, That

when

when he came firſt to his Kingdom, He knew not one *Prieſt* on the South ſide of the River *Humber*,that underſtood his Service in *Latine*, or that could Tranſlate an Epiſtle into Engliſh. *Vignier* in his *Eccleſiaſtical Hiſtory* affirms, That *Gerbertus* the firſt Archbiſhop of *Rhemes* and *Ravenna*, afterwards *Pope*, under the name of *Silveſter* the Second ,was reputed a *Magician*, becauſe he was well skill'd in the *Mathematicks.* (Thus, ſaith Dr. *Fuller*, ſo Ignorant People count all *Circles* above their own *Sphere* to be *Conjuring*, and preſently cry out, thoſe Things are done by the *Black Art*, for which their dim Eyes can ſee no Colour in reaſon. And in ſuch Caſes, when they cannot fly up to *Heaven* to make it a *Miracle*, they fetch it from *Hell* to make it *Magick*) And how low Learning ran in *England* amongſt the Native Nobility, in the Reign of King *Henry* the *Sixth*, too plainly appears by the *Motto* on the Sword of the *Martial*, Earl of *Shrewsbury*,

which

which was, *Sum Talboti, pro Occidere in imicos meos*, the beft Latin that Noble Lord, and perchance his Chaplains too (in that Age) could afford. *Erafmus* tells us, That fome Divines in his time undertook to prove, that *Hereticks* ought to be put to Death, from thofe Words of the Apoftle, *Hæreticum Hominem devita*, which it feems they underftood, as if he had faid, *De vitâ tolle*. I have read of two *Fryars* difputing Whether God had made any more *Worlds* than One; the One wifely alledging that paffage of the Gofpel touching the ten *Lepers* which were cleans'd, *Annon Decem facti funt Mundi?* As if God had made Ten Worlds ; the other (with great gravity) looking into the Text, replies as wifely, with the words immediately following, *Sed ubi funt Novem?* But what is become of the Nine? So as from thence he would prove but one to be left. An old Prieft in *Henry* the *Eight*'s time, being reprov'd for reading in his ServiceBook *Mumpfimus Domine,*
                                    inftead

inftead of *Sumpſimus*, reply'd, He had now us'd *Mumpſimus* theſe thirty Years, and for his part he would not leave his old *Mumpſimus* for their new *Sumpſimus*. At any time when their *Prieſts* were taken breaking *Priſcian's* head, their Common De-fence was, thoſe words of St. *Grego-ry*, *Non debent verba cæleſtis Oraculi ſubeſſe regulis Donati*, The words of the Heavenly Oracles ought not to be Subject to the Rules of *Donatus*. But theſe are Stories ſo well known, that I ought to Apologiſe for in-ſiſting ſo long upon them; and there-fore to proceed to the laſt *Queſtion.viz.*

Whether Men do now live to as great an Age, as they did formerly? It muſt be granted, That in the firſt Ages of the World, both before and for ſome time after the *Flood*, Men did generally arrive to a much grea-ter Age, than they have done ſince. But this is certainly to be attributed to ſome *extroardinary Cauſe*, and not to the *Ordinary Courſe of Nature*. The World (we know) was then to
be

be replenish'd with Inhabitants, which could not so speedily be done, but by an extroardinary Multiplication of Mankind ; Neither could that be done, but by the long lives of Men. And again, Arts and Sciences were then to be planted, for the better effecting whereof, it was requisite, that the same Men should have the Experience and Observation of many Ages. We know it was the Complaint of *Hippocrates, Ars longa, Vita brevis* ; And therefore Almighty God, in his Wisdom did then proportion Mens *Lives* to the length of *Arts :* And as God gave them this special Priviledge to live long ; so 'tis probable he gave them withal a Temper, and Constitution of Body, answerable thereunto. As also the *Food* wherewith they were nourish'd, especially before the *Flood,* may well be thought to have been more *wholesome* and *nutritive,* and the *Plants* more *Medicinal :* And happily the *Influence* of the *Heavens* was at that time,

in

in that Climate where the *Pa-*
triarchs liv'd, more benign and fa-
vourable. These (as far as we poor
Mortals can Conjecture) might be
the reasons, why Divine Providence
did affign to those firſt Inhabitants
ſo long a leaſe of their Lives. But in
after-times, when the World was
fully Peopl'd, and Arts and Sciences were Propagated, then it pleaſ'd
the ſame Divine Providence to cur-
tail, and abridge the Life of Man ;
inſomuch that in *Moſes*'s time the
common Standard of humane Life
was *Seventy*, or at moſt *Eighty Years*.
And ſo it was ever after counted.
Hence alſo *Herodotus* ſets the long-
eſt Bounds of Man's Life to be but
Eighty Years. *Barzillai* was ſaid to be a
very Old Man, and yet he liv'd but to
fourſcore : And *David* was full of
Days, yet but Seventy Years Old.
Solomon, as Divines Conjecture, was
not Sixty, yet it is ſaid, *when Solo-*
mon was Old. The Learned *Johannes*
Jonſtonius. tells us, That in all the
Records of the *Roman, Greek, French,*
and

and *German* Emperours, there were but four who liv'd to be fourscore. And our *English* Chronicle informs us, That Queen *Elizabeth* out-liv'd all her Predeceſſors from *William* the Conquerour. *Petrus Crinitus* ſaith, that the *Ægyptians* by a ſubtile Conjecture, taken from the Weight of the *Heart*, found out within what bounds the Life of Man was included; they affirming, That it was ſcarce poſſible for a Man to live above a Hundred Years : For, ſaid they, the *Heart* every Year till Fifty increaſed two *Drams*, and from thence to an hundred Years it decreaſed as much, and ſo returning to its original Weight, it can then make no further Progreſs. Now, though this Obſervation does certainly carry in it more of *Curioſity* than *Truth*, yet doth it plainly ſhew, That the common Opinion of the *Ancients*, was, That Men did ſeldom live above a Hundred Years. And we find, the Learned *Varro* was alſo of the ſame Belief, and there-

therefore he tells us, They call'd the space of a Hundred Years, *Seculum*, from *Senex*, an old Man, because they thought that was the utmost Period of Mans life. Thus then we see, That Men live now as long as they did formerly ; and that for these three Thousand Years at least there hath been no Alteration. It is the Observation of that great Philosopher, the Lord *Verulam*, *Decursus Seculorum*, & *Succeßio Propaginis, nihil videntur omnino demere de Diuturnitate vitæ* ; The Course of Times, and Succession of Ages, seem to have no whit abated from the length of Mens Lives. *No doubt*, says that Noble Lord, *There are times in all Countrys, wherein Men live either longer or shorter ; longer, most commonly when the Times are Barbarous, and the Diet more plain, and more given to bodily Exercise ; shorter, when they are more Civil, and there is more Luxury and Idleneß ; But in these Things there is a Vicißitude and Revolution ; The Suc-*

ceßion

cession of Generations alters it not. If it did, the first Man in reason should have lived longest, and the Son should still come short of his Fathers Age ; So that whereas *Moses* tells us, That the Days of Man in his time were Threescore Years and Ten, by this reckoning they might well enough by this time be brought to ten, or twenty, or thirty at the most. In a Word, we will not say, but that Accidents, Accidental Occurrences, Intemperance, ill and noxious Effluvia from the Earth, Waters, and intemperature of the Air, and other Accidents may in these latter Ages of the World produce some such Diseases, and accidental Disorders, as may possibly more infest Mankind, and occasion more Mortality, than in former Ages: But as to the regular and ordinary Course of Natural Procedure and State of Things with Mankind, yea and other Animals, there seems to be little or no decay, or Variation from what hath been formerly.   ESSAY VI.

ESSAY VI.

Of PASSION; *And whether the* PASSIONS *are an* Advantage, *or* Diſadvantage *to Men.*

TWAS the uſual ſaying of a very Ingenuous Perſon, *That Paſſionate Men, like Torkſhire Hounds, are apt to over-run the Scent.* They have not the Patience to pauſe and deliberate, but *Quicquid in Buccam venerit,* whatſoever they think they ſpeak; and therefore it is, they often run into ſuch groſs Abſurdities; for as *Ariſtotle* well obſerves, *Qui cito pronunciat, ad pauca reſpicit.* A mind tranſported with Paſſion, rejects the beſt Reaſons, and retains the

worſt

worſt Opinions; like a *Bolter*, which lets the *Flour* paſs, and keeps nothing but the *Bran*. Therefore *Plato* ſpeaking of *Paſſionate* Perſons, ſays, They are like Men who ſtand upon their Heads, they ſee all things the wrong way. How inconſiſtent *Paſſion* and *Reaſon* is, *Seneca* ſeems to intimate, by that Expreſſion of his *Nemo conſilium cum Clamore dat*: And how incompatible the Spirit of God and Paſſion is, the Holy Scriptures themſelves do plainly ſhew; For when *Elias* was upon the Mountain, there came a Whirlwind, and God was not there; then an Earthquake, and God was not there; But at laſt came a ſtill Voice, and God was there. The Scripture likewiſe exhorteth us, *To poſſeſs our Souls in Patience*; intimating, according to the Lord *Bacon's* Paraphraſe, *That whoſoever is out of Patience, is out of the Poſſeſſion of his Soul*; Well therefore might the Poets call *Anger a ſhort Madneſs*: For look upon an Angry Man, when he is in the height of of his Rage, and you may fee all *Africa*,. and its Prodigies in him: He is more favage than the Tygers there; Blow him into a Flame, and you may fee *Vulcano's, Hurricans*, and *Borafco's* in him. And certainly were he (while his Paſſion was thus raging) forc'd to look himſelf in the Glaſs, thoſe very Convulſions and Diſtortions his Anger had put him into, would ſoon ſhame him into a better temper. In ſhort, there is no ſurer Argument of a great Mind, than not to be tranſported to Anger by any Accident whatſoever; The Clouds and Tempeſts are form'd below, but all above is quiet and ſerene; which is the true Emblem of a Brave Man, that ſurpaſſes all Provocations, and Lives within himſelf. This made a great Philoſopher fay, That a Wiſe Man ought to be like the *Caſpian Sea*, which is ſaid never to *Ebb* or *Flow.* But from this exceſs of the Paſſions to infer an utter uſeleſſneſs of them, to me ſeems very unreaſo-

nable;

nable : For I cannot think Nature is such a severe Step-Dame, as that by her Planting these Passions in us, she design'd only to Plague and Torment us: I therefore conclude, There is an honest and an innocent use of them. As *Bias* once said of the Tongue, that it was the best and worst part of Man, so may we of the Affections ; *Nec meliores unquam servos, nec Dominos sentit Natura Deteriores,* They are the best Servants, but the worst Masters that Nature can have; like the Winds, which being moderate, carry the Ship ; but drown it, being tempestuous. And as it is observed in greater States, so does the same hold true in Man's little Common-wealth , that those who are the fittest for Service, if once they become Mutinous, always prove the most dangerous sort of Enemies : And thus the old Rule, *Corruptio Optimi Pessima,* holds true. I know there have been several Modern *Stoicks,* who with a *zeal* much transcending their *Knowledge,* have
declaim'd

declaim'd against the Passions ; Nothing less than an utter Extripation will satisfie these Men : They are not contented with our keeping them under, and retaining them upon the same terms, as *Abraham did those Domesticks he bought with his Money,* whom the Scriptures saith, *He both Circumcis'd, and kept as Servants* ; But they tell us, that the Mind ought to deal with its Affections, just as *Pharaoh* would have dealt with the *Jews-Males* , whom he thought it best to cut off, for fear they might (some time or other) be in a condition to make head against him. But whether this be reasonable or no, let any Man judge : Because the Passions are now and then diforderly, must we therefore wish there were no Passions ? No certainly ; for this would be every whit as unreasonable, as to wish there were no *Rivers* in the world, because it sometimes happens, that by their overflowing we receive great Detriment. When I consider, That

O 3 our

our Bleſſed Saviour, who took upon him all our *Natural* Infirmities, but none of our *Sinful*, has been ſeen to *Weep*, to be *Sorrowful*, to *Pity*, and to be *Angry* ; I cannot but than conclude, *That a Man may be Angry and Sin not.* It is not the bare Agitation, but the Sediment at the bottom that troubles and defiles the Water. The Paſſions are ſo far from being always hurtful, that we read of ſeveral that have receiv'd great advantages from them. For *Wit* proceeds from Active Spirits, or a good Degree of Heat in the Brain ; And therefore they, who have been deny'd by Nature this Faculty, and will not take the Pains by Study and Exerciſe to improve their Parts, do often times encreaſe their Heat by ſome high Paſſion, and ſo appear more Witty and Ingenious than at other times, when their Spirits (being as it were benumm'd with Cold) are not able to exert themſelves; And from hence came that known ſaying, *Vexatio dat Intellectum.*

telleɕum. *Seneca*, hearing a dull
Orator make a moſt Eloquent Harangue the very day his Son dy'd,
cry'd out, *Magna pars Eloquentiæ eſt
Dolor* ; ſo *Polus* the Actor, to enable
him to make a more lively Repre-
ſentation of the Grief of a Father
upon the Body of his Deceaſed Son,
brought in an *Urn* the Aſhes of
his own Son newly Dead. So much
for the Paſſion of Grief. Then for
Anger, *Si Natura negat, Facit In-
dignatio verſum.* *Archilochus* and
Hipponaux were two very indifferent
Poets, yet in meer Spleen and Malice, to be revenged of two Perſons
that had injur'd them, invented thoſe
Doggrel ſorts of Verſes, *Iambicks*
and *Scazons*, which they did to ſuch
a Perfection, that their Adverſaries
deſpairing of ever being able to an-
ſwer them, made away themſelves.
And as for the Paſſion of Love, let
the Smith of *Antwerp* paſs for an
Inſtance ; who being rejected by his
Sweet-Heart becauſe of his dirty
Profeſſion, chang'd his Hammers and

O 4 Anvil,

Anvil, for Pencils and Tables, and so from an Inconsiderable Black-Smith, he became the moft noted Painter of his time. Thus we fee, the Paffions, if rightly manag'd, are of great Ufe and Service to us; But if once we fuffer them to grow headftrong, Lions, Wolves, and Tygers are more governable. We too well know, there is not any one thing hath done more hurt to the Chriftian Religion, than the Spirit of Paffion ; as is moft evident by thofe many late unhappy Difputes and Controverfies amongft us. 'Tis ftrange, that Men cannot talk of Religion, but at the fame time they muft Quarrel too; as if the beft way of eftablifhing the Law of *God*, was by violating the Laws of *Charity*. I thank God my Charity is of an Extenfive Nature ; I refrain no man's Company, becaufe his Opinion comes not up to mine ; Nor do I think it reafonable, that a difference in Opinion fhould divide an Affection. Mens Underftandings are

not

not all of one Size and Temper;
and therefore it cannot be imagin'd,
there ever will be such a Consonan-
cy, and Uniformity of Judgment
amongst all Men, no, not amongst
Wise and Good Men, but that in
many things, yea and those sometimes of great Importance, they
may and will dissent one from another unto the Worlds end. But it
is one thing to *Dissent from*, and
another, to be at *Discord with*, a
Man : *Ita dissensi ab illo* (says *Tully*
concerning himself and *Cato*) *ut in
disjunctione sententiæ, conjuncti tamen
amicitiâ maneremus.* 'Tis an excellent
Rule saith Bishop *Wilkins*, *to be observ'd in all Disputes*, *That Men
should give soft words, and hard Arguments*: *That they should not so
much strive to vex, as to convince an
Enemy.* If this were but diligently
practis'd in all Cases, and on all
sides, we might in a good Measure
be freed from those vexations in the
search of Truth, which the Wise
Solomon, by his own Experience, did

fo much complain of, when he told us, That *in much Wifdom there is much Grief, and he that encreaf-eth Knowledge, encreafeth Sorrow.* There is nothing fo impertinent in Difputes and Controverfies, as Anger and Paffion: For every Man is fond of his own Notions, and no Man cares to be Huff'd and Hector'd out of it ; and therefore this Blufte-ring way is fo far from inclining us to yield to Mens Opinions, that it rather hardens us againft them, by giving us a prejudice to their Per-fons. For my part, I love to fpeak of *Perfons* with Civility, but of *Things* with Freedom ; and there-fore I abhor the Practice of Many, who write, as if they thought *Rai-ling* at any Mans Perfon, or Wrang-ling about his Words, neceffary to the Confutation of his *Opinions* ; Me-thinks, it is as unwife, as provoking ; for if I civilly endeavour to reafon a Man out of his *Opinions*, I make my felf but one Work to do, namely, to convince his Underftanding ; but

if

if in a bitter or exasperating Way, I
oppose his Errors, I encrease the
difficulties I wou'd surmount, and
have as well his *Affections* against
Me, as his *Judgment* : And it is very uneasie to make a *Proselyte* of
him, who not only differs from us,
but is an Enemy to us. Besides, as
a *Mad-Dog* by biting others, is wont
to make those he bites runMad like
himself; So, these *Provoking Writers*, are wont to enrage those they
offend, and infect them also with their
own virulent Distemper. In a Word
then, They are the Gentle Insinua-
tions which pierce, as Oil is the
most penetrating of all Liquors ;
And the best way of *Proselyting*
Men, is to gain their Affections.
If Disputes could be manag'd with
Temper and Moderation, Men might
certainly reap great benefit by them :
But our unruly Passions do so much
get the Ascendant over our Understandings, that this is a thing rather
to be wish'd, than to be expected.
Upon thisConsideration was it, That
the

the great *Montaign* was for fuppreffing and hindering all Difputes and
Controverfies : And much of the
fame Mind was the Philofopher *Plato*, who in his *Republick* prohibits
this Exercife to Fools and ill-bred
People. I think, there is not any
Man fo ignorant, but knows, That
nothing hath been a greater Scandal
to the Reformed Religion, either a-
mong *Heathens*, *Mahometans*, or
Papifts; nay, nor hath given a fairer
occafion for bringing in of Atheifm
and Infidelity, than our Divifions
and Animofities, which proceed from
our many Controverfies and Difputes
of Religion. Indeed, our Controverfies about Religion, faith the
Learned *Stillingfleet*, have brought
at laft even Religion it felf into a
Controverfie : For weaker heads,
faith he, when they once perceive
the Battlements fhake, are apt to
fufpect the Foundation it felf ftands
not firm; and if they fee any thing
call'd in Queftion, they prefently
conclude, there is nothing certain.
Luther,

Luther, obferving how prejudicial School-Divinity had been to the Chriftian Religion, crys out, *Quamprimum apparuit Theologia Scholaftica, evanuit Theologia Crucis.* The *School-Men* have fpun the *Thread* too fine, and made *Chriftianity* look liker a Courfe of *Philofophy*, than a *Syftem* of *Faith*, and *Supernatural Revelation* : So that the Spitit of it evaporates into Niceties and Exercifes of the Brain ; and the Contention is not for *Truth* but *Victory*. Indeed, when I confider the Works of the *School-Men*, it puts into my Thoughts, how far more importantly a good Method of *Thinking*, and a right Courfe of Apprehending Things, does contribute towards the attaining of Perfection in true Knowledge, than the ftrongeft and moft vigorous Wit in the World, can do without them. It cannot without Injuftice be deny'd, That they were Men of extraordinary ftrength of Mind : They had a great Quicknefs of Imagination, and Subtilty of Diftinguifhing : They very

very well underſtood the Conſequence of Propoſitions : Their Natural Endowments were Excellent :
Their Induſtry Commendable : But
they lighted on a wrong Path at
firſt, and wanted Matter to contrive ;
And ſo, like the *Indians,* only ex-
preſſed a wonderful Artifice, in the
ordering of the ſame Feathers into a
thouſand varieties of Figures. But
after all that can be ſaid in their
Commendation, we muſt needs own,
That nothing hath been of more
miſchievousConſequence to Chriſtian Religion than *School-Divinity*.
I know it is much controverted a-
mongſt the Learned, how this *School-*
Learning came firſt to be ſet up :
But to give *Ariſtotle* his due, I think
it may eaſily be prov'd, That he was
not the chief Author of this *So-*
phiſtick kind of Diſputation, which
now reigns in our *Schools,* but rather the *Arabians, Averroes* and *A-*
vicenna , his Commentators ; who
being wholly unacquainted with the
Greek Tongue, were fain to depend
upon

upon the *Versions* of *Aristotle*, which being very imperfect, left them under great Darkness and Ignorance touching *Aristotle's* Sense and Meaning; whence there sprang a world of *Unintelligible Terms*, and *Distinctions*, with as many *Sophistick Disputes* and *Controversies*. These the *School-Men* greedily lick'd up (as the *Minor Poets* what came from *Homer*) and incorporated with their *Theology*; which fill'd the Universities of *France*, (where this *School-Divinity* was first broach'd,) and *England* (which had continual Recourse to *Paris* for Learning) with nothing but vain λογομαχία, or strife about Words instead of solid *Phylosophy* and *Divinity*; far worse than what was to be found in the Pagan *Schools*. Which vain *Itch* of *Disputation* hath proved the *Scab* of the *Church*, as hath been observ'd by many Learned Men. When Men will be wiser than God, and in their foolish Wisdom think it fit to add their strength to Gods weakness, as a speedier and surer

way

way to eftablifh the Truth ; then does God, to convice them of their folly, fuffer ,that ftrong Man, the Enemy of the Gofpel, (whom none but his almighty Arm can bind and Mafter) to come, and fow his Tares of Divifion,which foon over-runs the good Seed of the Church, and fo brings all to Confufion.Thus then, by our foolifh Notions and Conceptions do we often ftain and dilute the very Fountain it felf. And as the *Jews* dealt with the Bleffed *Jefus*, fo do we now with his Holy Religion, by platting its head with a Crown of Thorns. And this is that, that hath robb'd the Chriftian World of its Unity and Peace, and made the Church the Stage of Ever-lafting Contentions. For nothing puts Men more out of humour one with another, than Schifms and un-neceffary Breaches of Church Com-munion: This naturally fours the Tempers of Men, and alienates their Affections to the higheft Degree ; for both Parties endeavouring to

vindicate

vindicate themselves, are forc'd to recriminate, and these Recriminations always end in Heat and Passion; And so, like two *Flints* struck together, they will be continually sparkling and spitting fire at one another, till they have kindled the Quarrel into an inquenchable Flame. It is the Learned *Selden's* Observation, That *Disputes* in *Religion* will never be ended, because there wants a *Measure*, by which the Business wou'd be decided. 'Tis just as if two Men were at Bowls, and both judg'd by the Eye: *One* says, 'tis his Cast, the *Other* says, 'tis my Cast; and having no *Measure*, the Dispute is Eternal. I remember, *Ben. Johnson* satyrically expresses the vain Disputes of *Divines* by *Inigo Lanthorn*, disputing with his *Puppet* in *Bartholomew Fair. It is so; It is not so; It is so; It is not so;* crying thus one to another a Quarter of an Hour together. Thus we see, how much even Religion suffers by these unhappy Disputes and Quarrels among

P us:

us: For there is nothing does more
abate the inward ſtrength of Religion, than when it is rarified into
Airy Notions and Speculations;
This (indeed) gnaws and conſumes
the very Vitals, and in a ſhort time
will quite deſtroy the ſubſtance of it.
It was the *Motto* of the Primitive
Chriſtians, *Non magna loquimur, ſed
vivimus,* our Religion conſiſts not
in *Talking,* but in *Doing* Great Things.
But may not the *Reverſe* of this be
properly apply'd to the Preſent
Age, *viz. Non vivimus, ſed Magna
Loquimur.* Religion is now become
one of the *Artes Sermocinales*, a
Talkative Myſtery, an Art not to
govern the *Mind*, and to regulate
the *Actions*, but to Frame and Fa-
ſhion *Diſcourſe*. The *Eſſence* and
being of *Chriſtianity* is *Practice*; and
according to that Teſt, where almoſt can it be ſaid to exiſt in the
World? 'Tis true we have ſome I-
mages and Shaddows of it: Some
have taken its Picture, but the Sub-
ſtance and Solid Body is vaniſh'd,
　　　　　　　　　　　　　re-

resolv'd into Air, and like the Fable
of the *Sybills* being worn into a
Voice, we have turn'd it into a
meer *Noise* and *Sound*; nay, which
is worse, into an *Eccho,* that flat-
tering complying Voice, which Re-
verberates every Mans own Language to him : Men dictate to their
Religion, and then will needs per-
suade Themselves and others, That
their *Religion* dictates to *them,* and
so will have the *Rebounds* of their
own Fancy pass for *Divine Oracles.*
And now to conculde, 'tis no wonder, that our Disputes and Controversies have so ill an effect, when
our unruly Passions have so great a
share in them. For, as we have said
before, the Passions if not modera-
ted, are the Brutish Part in us; and
therefore, when we transform our
selves into *Beasts,*it is not to be supposed we can Act like *Men.*

ESSAY VII.

ESSAY VII.

The Variety of OPINIONS : *Whence it proceeds : The uncertainty of Humane Knowledge.*

ALL our feveral *Opinions* are nothing but the meer various Tafts of feveral Minds, fram'd partly by our feveral Natures, partly by our different Educations, and Inftructions, and partly by the various Encounters, which we have met with in our ways of Life. Hence it is, that *Quot Homines, tot Sententiæ, Opinions* are as numerous as Mankind it felf ; and that the feveral Confti-rutions of our Minds, differ no lefs than thofe of our Bodies. There are as many Internal Forms of the Mind, as there are External Figures of Men: And the Soul of Man hath its Palat, as well as the Body; *Opinion* being nothing but the Gufto or Relifh of the Soul: Nay, fome have been fo Critical, as to affirm, That there is fo great a Correfpondence betwixt the one and the other, that thofe who are of a different Diet, are generally obferv'd to be of different Opinions; and the Learned Dr. *Harvey* gives this for the reafon, Becaufe (fays he) a different Diet fends up different *Steams* to the Head, and according to thefe *Steams* are Mens *Opinions*. But this founding more like a *Notion* than a *Truth*, we fhall lay no ftrefs upon it, but proceed. There is (then) a certain Congruity of fome Opinions to the particular Tempers of fome Men; and therefore we fee, how readily fuch Doctrines, as fuit themfelves to the particular Inclination of the Mind, or Underftanding, are

embraced

embraced, and received; whereas thofe that are oppofite to it, are commonly rejected with the greateft contempt imaginable. Thus do we Love, and Hate without being able to give a Reafon why. Some Faces both of Perfons, and Things, we admire and doat on; to others, much better deferving our efteem, we can fcarcely afford a common Civility. Indeed, the dull and unactive Spirits, that concern not themfelves in *Theory*, do feldom take the trouble to examine Matters, but taking Things in the Grofs, follow the Common Belief, and are for keeping the beaten Road; But thofe, whofe Minds are of a Brifker, and more Vigorous Conftitution, will fall into that of their particular *Crafis*. Hence then, I fay, is it, we find Men taking in fome particular *Opinions* with ftrange Pleafure and Satisfaction, upon their very firft Propofals; when at the fame time they will not hearken to others, though they recommend themfelves with a much greater ftrength of Reafon.

Reafon. Thus it is eafie to diftinguifh in moft Men, two Sorts of *O-
pinions*; *Opinions* that grow upon
Mens Complexions, and *Opinions*
that are the Refults of their Reafon;
and we meet with very few, that are
of a Temperament fo equal, or a
Conftitution fo even poifed, but
that they encline to one fet of *Opinions* rather than another, antece-
dently to all proofs of Reafon ;
And when they have efpoufed their
Opinions from that fecret *Sympathy*,
then they find out as good Reafons
as they can to maintain them, and
fay, nay think fometimes, that 'twas
for the fake of thofe Reafons, that
they firft embraced them. But we
may commonly diftinguifh thefe *In-
clination-Opinions* from the *Rational*,
becaufe we find them accompanied
with more *Heat* than *Light*, a great
deal of eagernefs and impatience in
defending of them, and but flen-
der Arguments. In a Word, almoft
every one is fatisfied, That there is
a particular Genius, or fpecial In-

P 4   clination

clination in Mens Minds, and that some *Opinions* do naturally make a much greater impreffion than others; but the *vexata Quæftio* is, how, or from whence this *Temperament* of the *Mind* proceeds. Some therefore tell us, That this great Diverfity of the Operations of the Mind, is to be afcribed to the Souls Dependance upon the Body, and that a Good, or Bad Difpofition of the *Organical Parts*, does certainly render the Soul either Vigorous or Unactive in its feveral Operations. Whatfoever defect (then) we may perceive in fome Men, we are not to think it proceeds from any Deficiency in the Soul, but from the Coexiftence it has with a Body ill difpos'd for Affiftance and Information. For he who is carried in a Coach, (as the Body is *Vehiculum Animæ*) though he himfelf could go much fafter, muft yet receive fuch Motion as that affords ; And Water, which is convey'd through Pipes and Aqueducts, though its Motion by it felf

would

would have been otherwife, muft
yet then be confin'd and limited by
the Pofture and Proportion of the
Veffels through which it paffes.
Hence we are told, That fome Men
are even by Nature, and Complexion, inclin'd to Vertue and Goodnefs; as it was faid of *Clitus,*
(whom *Alexander* in a Drunken
humour flew,) *That he had Vertues*
by Nature, and Vices by Accident;
And that others, even by the odd-
nefs of their particular Make and
Contexture, are determin'd to Actions of Vice. It was a received O-
pinion among the Ancients, That
outward Beauty, was an infallible
Argument of inward Beauty; and
fo on the contrary, That a deformed Body was a true Index of a deformed Mind, or an ill Nature.
Hence was that of the Poet:

Clauda tibi mens eſt, ut pes: Natura
   notaſque
Exterior certas Interioris habet.

As alſo that of *Martial, Lib.* 12.
Epigram 54.

Crine ruber, niger ore, brevis pede,
   lumine lœſus :
Rem magnam præſtas, Zoile, ſi bonus
   es.

It was alſo the ſaying of *Victori-*
nus, In diſtorta Membra virtus cade-
re non poteſt : And *Pythagoras* was
ſo bigotted to this Opinion, that
he would never admit into his
School any that had the leaſt Natural Blemiſh or Deformity. Upon
this general Opinion was grounded
that common Saying, *Cave tibi ab*
iis, quos Natura Signavit, which we
may render thus, *Whom God hath*
Markt, let Man Mark. And therefore
Homer, ſpeaking of the ſeveral ill
Qualities of *Therſites,* takes care to fit
him with a Body ſuitable to ſuch a
Mind. Now, the reaſon (poſſibly)
why Nature for the moſt part orders it ſo, may be this; the Method
ſhe takes (though imperceptible to
                                    us)

us) is Regular and Mathematical, and therefore probably nothing may more break and diforder that Symmetry fhe obferves, than by matching a good Soul with a deformed Body; for this feems to be *Impar Congreffus,* puting things unequally together. But yet this Rule is not fo general, as to admit of no Exception, as we may fee in the Emperour *Galba,* a Prince of an unhappy outward Figure, of whom it was faid, *Ingenium Galbæ malè habitat*; The fame may be alfo obferved of *Agefilaus,* and fome others, (though not many;) and therefore *Seneca* tells us, '*Ex cafâ vir Magnus exire poteft, & ex deformi humilique Corpufculo formofus Animus & Magnus.* I grant indeed, feveral Examples there are of Great Perfons, whofe outward Deformities have been very remarkable, and yet we find their Vertues and good Qualities highly celebrated; But yet (poffibly) did we but make a narrow fearch into their Lives, we fhould find the difference and alteration was chiefly

wrought

wrought by Education or Cuftom, which often-times over-fways Nature. Thus we fee, what a great Correfpondency there is betwixt the Soul and the Body, which is fuch, that they manifeftly participate the Affections one of the other : And therefore if the Body be fick, the Soul is alter'd in it's Operations, as we fee in high Fevers, and other acute Difeafes : And on the contrary, let the Soul be fad or joyful, the Body is fo too. Therefore the Sophifters of old were wont to Purge themfelves with *Hellebore* ; when they would difpute beft. For though in its Effence the Soul depends not on the Corporeal Organs, yet it depends upon the fame in its Operations, which are different according to the diverfe ftructures of the Organs ; which, if they were alike difpos'd; their Actions would be alike in all, and at all times. Whence faith *Ariftotle*, if an old Man had a young Mans Eyes, he would fee as clear as a Young Man. That Ingenious Mafter of Poetry, Mr.

Mr. *Dryden,* speaking of the mutability of *Man,* says, That our Minds are perpetually wrought on by the temperament of our Bodies : Which (saith he) makes me suspect, they are nearer ally'd, than either our Philosophers, or School-Divines will allow them to be. I have observ'd, says *Mountaign,* That when the Body is out of Order, its Companion is seldom at ease : An ill Dream, or a CloudyDay, has power to change this wretched Creature, who is so proud of a *Reasonable Soul,* and make him think to day what he thought not yesterday. The Learned Dr. *Henry More* says, *That our Imagination alters, even as our Blood and Spirits are alter'd; And therefore,* says he, *as Dreams are the Fancies of those that sleep, so Fancies are but the Dreams of Men awake; And these Fancies by day, as those Dreams by Night, will vary and change with the Weather, and present Temper of the Body.* Thus experience shews us, That sudden changes of *Weather* do often affect the Brain :

This

This disturbs the Imagination, and gives a new and Melancholy Complection to the Appearances of things. Some Men can scarcely talk *Sense*, unless the Sun shines out, a Cloud is enough to discompose 'em, and they rise and fall with the *Mercury* in the *Weather Glaß*. But to proceed; Others are of Opinion, that this great Diversity proceeds from another Cause, to wit, from the *Climat*. *Peter Heylin,* speaking of the Dispersion of the Families of the *Sons* of *Noah,* says, That though they all descended from one Common Root, yet by the Situations of their several Dwellings, they came to be of several Tempers and Affections; in which they were so different from one another, that they seem'd rather to have been made at first out of several Principles, than to have been deriv'd from one Common Parent. The Ground or Reason of which difference (says *Heylin*) is to be attributed to the different Tempers of those Countries in which they liv'd, and to the different Influences

Influences of the Heavenly Bodies on thofe feveral Countreys ; which do continue ftill the fame, though many times the Countreys fhift and change their old Inhabitants. Thus, if we enquire into the old Characters, which either *Florus*, *Cæfar*, *Tacitus*, or *Juvenal* gave of the old *Britains*, *Gauls*, *Germans*, *Normans*, &c. We fhall find that the fame Vertues, and Vices, do ftill profper under the fame Climats, notwithftanding in moft of thefe Places the old Inhabitants, or their Breed, are quit wore away. 'Tis obferv'd, That where the Heaven is always in the fame Pofture, as toward the *Poles* ; or where the Sun heats almoft in the fame Degree, as near the *Equator*, (which makes the Days and Nights equal,) the Manners and Inclinations of the People are alfo equal : And on the contrary, Thofe that by the feveral Remotions and Approaches of the Sun have different Conftitutions of *Air*, receive fuitable impreffions from the fame, which are afterwards manifefted in their Actions.

Actions. As (therefore) Fruits and Beasts differ according to the several Countries, in which they are ; so are Men born more or less Warlike, Just, Temperate, and the like, according to their several *Climats*. And therefore *Plato* thankt God, That he was an *Athenian*, and not a *Theban*. *Plutarch* tells us, That those of the higher part of the City of *Athens* were of a quite contrary humour to those that dwelt about the Gate of *Pyreus*; and it is observ'd, that those who dwell on the North-side of a Mountain, differ as much from those that dwell on the South side, as they do both from those in the Valley. Now, from this Diversity of Mens Tempers, proceed the several Forms, and Constitutions of Government ; and thence it is, that in the same Countreys we find little Variation as to Government; but that in all Ages they have still kept to much one and the same Form ; the same Genius or Temper ever continuing under the same *Climat* : And whenever any

Country

Country, either by perſwaſion, have voluntarily, or by force, have been compell'd to quit their old Form of Government: yet in proceſs of Time they naturally return into the old Channel. This then is the reaſon, why thoſe who inhabit the moſt Intemperate Climes, are always for preferring the Deſpotick, Arbitrary Rule; whereas thoſe who live under the more temperate, and leſs ſevere Climats, eſpecially in *Europe*, have affected and preferr'd more gentle & moderate Governments, running anciently much into Common-Wealths, and of latter Ages into Principalities, circumſcrib'd by Laws, which differ not ſo much in Nature as in Name. The natural reaſon whereof, ſays that Accompliſh'd Author, *Sir William Temple*, I take to be this, *viz. That in the more Intemperate Climates, the Spirits either exhal'd by Heat, or compreſſ by Cold, are render'd faint and ſlaggiſh and by that reaſon the Men grow tamer and fitter for Servitude: That in more temperate Regions, the Spirits are*

Q   *ſtronger*

stronger and more active, whereby Men become bolder in the Defence or Recovery of their Liberties. Now by what we have already said, it plainly appears, That the great Variety of Mens Actions and Opinions cannot proceed from the Diversity of their Souls, which are accounted all equal, but from that of their Bodies ; wherein according to the various Tempers thereof, the Soul produces that variety of Manners. Let us not then any longer wonder, to find so great a Diversity of Opinions in the World ; since it is a thing wholly impossible for all Men to be of the same mind : For so long as Mens Organs are of several makes, and we live under divers Climats, we must necessarily have different Sentiments, and Apprehensions of things. Nor would there be any harm in this Diversity of Opinions, could Men but divest themselves of that Pride and Arrogance, which makes them so fond of Propagating their own Notions. But while every Man pretends to
the

the *Spirit of Infallibility*, and muſt be a *Dictator* to the reſt of Mankind, then there is nothing but Confuſion and Diſorder to be expected. And this was that, which made ſuch Diſturbance, and Embroilments amongſt us in the late times : Every Opinion was made an Article of Faith, and every Article became a Ground of a Quarrel, and every Quarrel made a Faction, and every Faction was Zealous, and all Zeal pretends for God, and whatſoever is for God cannot be too much ; and indeed, we were come to that paſs, That we thought we lov'd not God, unleſs we hated our Brother, and that we had not the Vertue of Religion, unleſs we perſecuted all Religions but our own. But let us not deceive our ſelves, for, whatſoever ſome may think, this is not the violence that gains *Heaven*; Nor is there any thing that makes us more unlike God, who is the Father of Mercies, and the God of all Conſolation, than a Furious, Hot, and Perſecuting Spi-

Q 2

rit:

fit. His apprearance was in the soft and still Voice, not in Whirlwinds and Hurricanes; and where there is *Spiritus Procellæ*, we may satisfie our selves it proceeds from another Principle. The *Holy Ghost* was pleas'd to appear not in the Form of a *Vultur*, (a ravenous and devouring Creatur) but in the shape of a *Dove*, the Emblem of *Meekneß*. The true Church is styl'd by the name of the *Lilly amongst Thorns* : The *Lilly* does not *Scratch* and *Tear*, that's the Property of *Thorns* and *Briars*, the most inconsiderable sort of shrubs. (And indeed, let us but reflect who were the chief Promoters of our late Persecutions, and we shall find they were the slightest of the *Clergy*, and the most Profligate of the *Laity* : None being so fit to make Shipwrack of other Mens Consciences, as those who have none of their own.) The most natural and effectual way (then) of Promoting the Blessed Gospel, is, by following its own Rules, and Precepts of Meekness and Moderation. Sweet-

ness

nefs and Ingenuity will more command Mens Minds, than Paffion,
Sournefs, and Severity : As the foft
Pillow fooner breaks the Flint, than
the hardeft Marble. Therefore
when we would convice Men of a-
ny Error by the ftrength of Truth,
we fhould do it with all the tender-
nefs, and in the moft obliging manner we are able. For Truth and
Love are two the moft Charming
Things in the World ; and when
thefe go hand in hand together,
there is no Humane Force can with-
ftand them. But that which proves
very mifchievous to many, is their
taking that to be *Zeal* for God and
Religion, which really is nothing
but their own violent and furious
Paffion. True Zeal then is a fweet,
Heavenly, and gentle Fame, which
makes us active for God, but always
within the Sphear of Love. It never calls for *Fire from Heaven*, to
Confume thofe who agree not with
us in all Points and Circumftances.
It is much of the Nature of that

Q 3   kind

kind of *Lightning*, (that the Philosophers tell us of) which melts the
Sword within, but never singeth the
Scabard: It strives to save the Soul
but at the same time hurteth not
the Body. In a word, we may
learn what kind of *Zeal* it is we
should make use of in promoting
the Gospel, by an Emblem of Gods
own, given us in the Scriptures,
those *Fiery Tongues*, which upon the
Day of *Pentecost* sat upon the *Apostles*; and that these were Innocent
Flames, no Man can doubt, for we
do not find, that they did so much
as singe an hair of their heads.
This then is *true Zeal*, and whatsoever is more than this, proceeds
from evil, and is no other than a
Fever in the Soul. There is not
any thing that drives Men more
furiously, nor that hath more di-
sturb'd the Peace of Mankind, than
Mistaken Zeal. *Odia Religionum sunt
acerbissima*, is now grown into a
Proverb; of all Hatreds, there are
none more furious and unnatural,
than

than thofe which arife out of Contrarieties in Religion ; and it is generally obferv'd, That the lefs Material their Difference, the more implacable is theHatred : As the *Turks* think it more acceptable to God, to kill one *Perfian*, than feventy Chriftians. Nothing fo vehemently alienates Mens Affections,as variety of Judgment in matters of Religion ; Here they cannot difagree, but prefently they muft fall together by the Ears ; and when once Religion divides Mens minds, no other common Intereft can unite them ; and where Zeal diffolves Friendfhip, the ties of Nature are not ftrong enough to reconcile it : And therefore our Saviour tells us, That in this Cafe Men would forget all the Bonds of Natural Obligation ; infomuch that the Father would deliver up his own Child, and the Children their Parents unto Death : As we find, that the Bloody Hatred of *Cain* againft *Able* arofe from the different Acceptance of their Sacrifice. Nor

Q 4 indeed

indeed is it to be wonder'd, if that enmity grow exceffive, which hath zeal to kindle it, and pretence of Religion to warrant it: For when that which fhould reftrain, and fet limits to a Paffion, is made a Party to engage it, and fuel to foment it, no wonder if a Paffion, which hath no Bounds from Religion, do impofe none upon it felf. And this occafion of mutual Hatred, we find obey'd even in the ridiculous Superftitions of *Ægypt*, when one Town would kill and eat the Flefh of another, in zeal to the Calves, or Sheep, or other Creatures, which they did feverally worfhip. Now, having fhew'd how much mifchief *Miftaken Zeal* has done in the World, I need not fpend much time in fhewing the ill Succefs that Perfecution hath conftantly been attended with; the Hiftory of all Ages has done this to my hand. *Sanguis Martyrum, femen Ecclefiæ*, is a Truth will laft to the Worlds End. For there is fcarce any Man fo void of Huma-

Humanity, but hath good Nature
enough to compaſſionate thoſe that
are in miſery, and at the ſame time
to ſhew their abhorrence to the Authors of ſuch Cruelties: And therefore, no wonder that Perſecution
doth rather encreaſe, than leſſen
the number of *Martyrs*: For as it
gives moſt Men a prejudice to the
Perſecuting Party, ſo it enclines them
to commiſerate the *Suffering* Party ;
and this kindneſs to their *Perſons*,
does often terminate in the favour-
ing their *Opinions*. How prepoſterous then is it in any State, or Government, to endeavour to force their
Subjects to Unity in Religion ;
when, alas ! The experience of all
Ages ſhews how impracticable the
Thing is. 'Tis true, a State may
ſometimes force all its Subjects, to
ſubmit to an outward Uniformity
in all Things that concern Divine
Worſhip ; but yet they muſt know,
that every publick Diſturbance in
the Commonwealth, breaks all thoſe
Bonds aſunder of diſſembled Obedience,

dience, and that such Compulsions do both beget and ripen all Disorders. Thus we see, that it is Mens being so fond of their own Opinions, which gives the greatest disturbance to Mankind; and while we are so highly conceited of our own Parts and Abilities, it cannot be otherwise. Now the only cure for this sort of Vanity, is to reflect upon the uncertainty of Humane Knowledge. *Wisdom* is a *Gift*, that comes from above; 'tis a Talent that few are trusted with. *Fools* will always be the greater Number. *Wise* Men are like *Timber-Trees* in a Wood, but thin planted in the World, here and there One. We see in all *Greece* there were but Seven. A *Plurality* of *Voices*, 'tis true, carries the Question in all our Debates, but rather as an Expedient for *Peace*, than any Eviction of *Right*. Take the World throughout, and you will find a Thousand *Blockheads* to one *Wise* Man; *Flies* breed in Swarms, but *Lions* do not come into

to the world by *Litters*. There is
Folly (then) in all the Sons of Men,
They know but a very fmall part of
the Things that are in the World;
and thofe things they do know,
they know but in part. And befides their natural Ignorance, what
thro' Precipitancy, Mifinformation,
Prejudice, Partial Affections, and
feveral other Caufes, they are fubject to many grofs Miftakes and
Errors: Whereby it cometh to pafs,
That the *Wifeft* Men fometimes
are fouly over-feen, and are fain to
take up the *Fool's* Plea, and to cry,
Non putaram, Who *cou'd have thought
it*?

There is no Head fo found or
ftrong, but hath fome foft Place,
nor is any Mans Underftanding fo
perfect and fo clear, as to have
no *Flaw*, nor *Dark Water* in it.
The *French* tell us, That every
Man hath his *Foible*, his Blind or
Weak fide, and that there is no Man
fo *Wife*, but hath more or lefs of
the *Fool* in him. Every Man hath
fome-

something whereby he may be taken; and it is hard to find that *Fish*, that at some time or other will not bite, if the Bait be such as likes him. *One* Man is transported out of his Reason, and his Honesty, by sensual Pleasures ; *Another* by Money, perhaps, or by Ambition: Every Man, in short, by Somewhat or Other: And it is but striking him in the right Vein, to do his Business. Men are every jot as easily impos'd upon as *Birds*, *Beasts*, or *Fishes*; while the Eagerness of our Appetites suspends the Exercise of our Reason. A *Treat*, a *Woman*, or a *Bottle* is the same thing to us, that a *Worm*, a *Gudgeon*, a *Grain* of *Corn*, or a *Piece* of *Flesh* is to these Animals: We snap at the *Bait*, without ever dreaming of the *Hook*, the *Trap*, or the *Snare*, that goes along with it. Upon these Considerations therefore was it, That these several Sentences were grounded ; *Nemo Mortalium omnibus Horis Sapit*—— *Auriculas Asini Quis non habet ?* ——
Stulto-

*Stultorum plena funt Omnia——Quif-que fuos patimur Manes——*All which fayings, are but different *Phrafes* and *Dialects* to exprefs the Frailty and Imperfection of Humane Know-ledge The reafon then, why wife Men do never appear fo peremptory, and Dogmatical as others, is, becaufe they very well know, there are but few things fo certain, as to create much boldnefs, and confidence of Opinion. It was probably upon this Confideration, that the wife *Romans* fhew'd fo much Modefty, when they gave their Sentiments and O-pinions, concluding ftill for the moft part with thefe two words, *ITA VIDETUR.* 'Tis the Obfervati-on of the witty *Mountaign, That as amongft wife Men he is the wifeft, that thinks he knows leaft ; So amongft Fools he is the greateft, that thinks he knows moft.* Humane Nature is very fallible, the wifeft of Men do fometimes err, and therefore at the very Inftant a Man feems moft po-fitive, how does he know but he

may be *moſt Miſtaken ?* Do not e-
ven our very Senſes ſometime deceive us ? And yet moſt of our
Conceptions are taken from the
Senſes, and we can ſcarce judge
of any thing but by the help of
Material Images, that are thence
convey'd to us, according to that
old Rule, *Nihil eſt in Intellectu,
Quod non fuit priùs in ſenſu,* Since
therefore our Senſes are ſo very
fallacious, and from them reſult
moſt of Humane Knowledge, how
fond and ridiculous is it in any
Man to pretend to ſuch an Aſſurance ? *Eſt in ipſis rebus Obſcuritas,
& in judiciis noſtris Infirmitas,* ſaith
Tully ; ſo ſlight a Thing is Humane
Knowledge, That the moſt inconſiderable, and minuteſt Works of
Nature, ſerve to Puzzel, and Con-
found it. *Plato* ſays, That in Man
there is no ſuch Thing as *Science*
or *Knowledge,* 'tis but barely *Opinion :* and in another place he calls
Opinion, a Middle Thing betwixt
Ignorance and *Knowledge,* Indeed,
while

while we are in this World, we do
but behold by the favour of a Glim-
mering-Light, the Phantaſms and
Shadows of Things, which Cuſtom
makes us take forBodies andTruths:
All *Humane Knowledge*(then)is defe-
ctive:As it is,it is but *leſſer folly*;which
hitting ſometimes,fails asOften.And
as the*Fools Bolt* does not alwaysMiſs,
ſo the Wiſe Mans *Counſels* do not
always proſper. The beſt Knowledge a Man hath, is but a dim
ſort of Light ; which makes us apt
to Stumble, and often puts us to
grope out our Way. Our cleareſt
day here is Miſty and Hazy : We
ſee not far, and what we do ſee
is in a bad light. In a Word, we
may properly be ſaid to ſee the
wrong ſide of the *Hangings* ; and
let us pretend to what we will, the
utmoſt of *Humane Knowledge,* is but
a fair and Hopeful Conjecture.

Through

Through Seas of *Knowledge*, we
our Courfe advance,
Difcovering ftill new Worlds of
Ignorance ;
And thefe Difcoveries make us
all Confefs,
That *Sublunary Science* is but
Guefs.
Matters of Fact to Man are only
known,
And what feems more, is mere
Opinion.

Sir *JOH. DENHAM.*

Our Demonftrations are raifed upon Principles of our own, not of Univerfal Nature; and, as the Lord
Bacon notes, *We take up Opinions,*
fuitable rather to the Analogy of our
felves, than that of the Univerfe.
How unreafonable then are thofe
Men, who are fo pofitive and dogmatical in their own Opinions, that
rather than admit of the leaft Con-
tradiction, chufe to make the whole
World an *Aceldama* and a *Babel?*
And

And thus, have we not by fad Experience found it moſt true; That all the Miſeries, which have attended the variety of Opinions ſince the Reformation, have proceeded from this Grand Miſtake, the making our own private Opinions the Standard of infallible Truth ? Whereas all wiſe Men ought to conſider, That truth is a Thing not certainly known; Nay poſſibly, the All-Wiſe God thinks it too dazling a Thing for the Eyes of us poor Mortals, and therefore reſerves it for our Glorified Faculties.

R   ESSAY VIII.

ESSAY VIII.

An ESSAY of RELIGION.

THAT Idea which moſt Men have of *God*, is nothing elſe but a Picture of their own Complexions, juſt as the *Ethiopians* pictur'd their *Gods* Black, becauſe they were Black themſelves. And therefore we commonly obſerve, That ſuch as are of a four, moroſe Nature, are very apt to frame to themſelves a *God* of their own Temper. Thus do theſe Men vainly imitate the Power of the *Almighty*; who as he at firſt was pleas'd to make *them* after his Image, ſo wou'd they now make *him* after theirs. In this Manner do

ws

We Model all that is in *God* to our ownFancies ,and inftead of Believing him what he is, we even make him what we wou'd have him : Like *Micha*, we make us a *God* for our own peculiar Ufe, and form the *Deity* we intend to Worfhip. This then is the reafon, that we many times reprefent *God* in fuch falfeColours,and fo utterly unlike *Himfelf*;for out of an unreafonable partiality to our felves, we firft miftake the Deformities of our own Natures for Perfections, and then Deifie them into *Divine Attributes.* And thus many times it comes to pafs, that our Notions of *God*, are nothing but the Images of *our Selves*, which *Narciffus* like we fall in love with, for no other Reafon, but becaufe they reflect our own dear likenefs. But let us not deceive our felves, for whatever our little , narrow Conceits may be, ftill *God* is the fame, and will for ever keep up that Character, *I am that I am.* We can therefore no more alter the

R 2 true

true Nature of *God* by our Wild and extravagant Reprefentations of him, than a Deforming *Optick Glaſs* can the Object it difguifes. But certainly of all Sorts of Men, none do more miftake the *Divine Nature*, and by confequence do greater Mifchief to *Religion*, than thofe who wou'd perfwade us, That to be truly *Religious*, is to renounce all the Pleafures of Humane Life; As if *Religion* were a *Caput Mortuum*, a heavy, dull, infipid thing; that has neither Heat, Life, nor Motion in it : Or were intended for a *Meduſa's* Head to transform Men into Monuments of Stone. Whereas (really) *Religion* is of an Active Principle, it not only elevates the Mind, and invigorates the Fancy; but it admits of Mirth, and pleafantnefs of Converfation, and indulges us in our Chriftian Liberties; and for this reafon, fays the Lord *Bacon, It is no leſs impious to ſhut where God Almighty has open'd, than to open where God Almighty has ſhut.*

But,

But, I fay, if Men will fuffer themfelves to be thus impos'd upon, as
to Believe, That *Religion* requires
any fuch unneceffary Rigours and
Aufterities, all that can be faid,
is, The fault does not lye in *Religion*, but in their *Underftandings* ;
Nor is this to paint *Religion* like
herfelf,but rather like one of the *Furies* with nothing but Whips and
Snakes about her. And fo, they
Worfhip *God* juft as the *Indians* do
the *Devil*, not as they love him,
but becaufe they are afraid of him.
It is not therefore to be wonder'd,
that fince their Notions of *God* are
fuch; their Way of Worfhip is a-
greeable thereunto ; And hence it is,
That thefe Men ferve *our* God, juft
as fome Idolaters Worfhip *theirs* ;
with painful Convulfions of Body,
and unnatural Diftortions of Face ,
and all the difmal folemnities of a
gloomy Soul, and a dejeted Countenance. Now thefe are the Men,
who upon all Occafions are fo apt
to condemn their Brethren, and, as

if

if they were of God's *Cabinet Coun-cel*, pretend to know the *Final De-crees* of the *Almighty*. But alafs *!* who is fufficient for thefe Things *?* Certainly, no Man can render him-felf more foolifhly ridiculous, than by meddling with thefe *Secrets* of *Heaven*. The *Decrees* of *God* we fay are *Hidden*, but in the fame breath we contradict our felves, and endeavour to Confute that *E-pithet*, by pretending to know them. Methinks our Ignorance in the Crea-tures, and being fo far at a lofs as to flie to *Occult Qualities*, which *Scaliger* calls *Ignorantiæ Afylum*, fhou'd check our Curiofity in the Things of God, and teach us to fit down Contented to refolve Gods Actions into fome *Hidden Caufes*. The Heathen *Seneca* cou'd fay, *Nun-quam Verecundiores debemus effe quàm cùm de Deo Agitur*, Modefty never becomes us better, than when we fpeak of God, *qui ut intelligatur ta-cendum eft*, as *Arnobius* elegantly expreffes it, which feems to agree
with

with that of the *Apostle*, who ad-
vises us *to become Fools, that we may
be Wise.* Secular states, we see, do
with a great deal of Jealousy reserve
their *private Councels* ; and shall we
think *God* so scrutable, or our selves
so penetrating that none of his *Secrets* can escape us ? Or if we think
him, as indeed he is, unfathomable,
why do we thus madly attempt what
we confess impossible ? Especially
since we shall not only lose the
thing we so vainly pursue, but
others we might else enjoy. God
has given us Rules of Life, which
upon the severest Penalties he requires us to study and practice ;
but alas! This we make no part of
our Business, and most of our time
is taken up in unfolding the *impene-
trable Counsels* of *Heaven.* I have
read of a *Philosopher,* who not mind-
ing his way, but gazing upon the
Stars, happen'd to fall into a Ditch :
Even so is this much our Case ;
while we are prying into the *Stars*
to read our *Destiny,* and do not re-

gard

gard the neceſſary Duties of *Reli-gion*, we do thereby fall into the *Worſt Fate* they could have portend-ded : And, for my part, I firmly Believe, That the Extravagant No-tions ſome Men have had concern-ing Gods *Decrees*, have reprobated more than thoſe *Decrees* upon which they are ſo willing to charge their Ruine. And, indeed, it is but juſt and reaſonable it ſhould be ſo ; for if Men will at this rate tranſcend the Bounds of Modeſty, and uſurp God'sPrerogative,they very well de-ſerve to meet with their ownDeſtru-ction. That *Ark* which devoutly reverenced, brought *Bleſſings*, when curiouſly pry'd into, diffus'd *Peſti-lence* and *Death*. Nay, the very *Poets* will tell us, That if we will have *Prometheus's* Fire, we muſt take *Pandora's* Box alſo : And ſure In-duſtry cannot be worſe laid out,than thus to fetch home Plagues to our ſelves. Let us then be contented to act within our own Sphear, and no longer ſoar after things*Inſcrutable*
and

and paſt finding out : Let us learn
contentedly to be ignorant, where
God wou'd not have us knowing;
nor think it any diſparagement to ac-
knowledge ſome *Depths* in God,
which our ſhallow Reaſon cannot
Fathom. *Næ intelligendo faciunt,*
ut nihil intelligant ; the way to make
our ſelves meer Fools, is to affect
to know more than God would
have us. Juſt as he who affects to
pry into the Body of the Sun, by
gazing grows ſtark Blind, and ſees
leſs then otherwiſe he might by thoſe
ſcatter'd Rays in the Air. In a
Word, it is the Glory of our *Reli-*
gion, that we accknowledge ſuch a
God as is unſearchable.

And as *Religion* teaches us *Mo-*
deſty, ſo does it likewiſe incline
Men to *Meekneß* and *Goodneß of Na-*
ture. Of all Vertues and Digni-
ties of the Mind *Goodneß of Nature*
(ſays *Bacon*) is the greateſt, being
the very Character of the *Deity* :
And without it *Man* is a Buſie, Miſ-
chievous,

chievous, wretched thing; no better than a kind of *Vermin*.

· The *Heathen* speaking of *God*, usually stile him by two Attributes, *Optimus & Maximus*, the one importing his *Goodness*, the other his *Power* ; but we see the Precedency is given to his *Goodness*, it being *that* wherein *God* himself is most delighted ; and therefore all the Acts of our *Saviour*, while he convers'd on Earth among Men, were purely the effects of, and emanations from, his *tenderness* and *Good Nature.* Tho' all God's *Attributes* are *Infinite*, yet this Beloved, Triumphant Attribute of his, his *Mercy*, transcends the rest ; and therefore (if it were possible) he seems herein to be somewhat more than *Infinite.* *Tertullian* Observes, that the Prime Quality in God is *Goodness*; this (saith he) is Natural and Eternal ; but his *Severity* is casual and adventitious ; the one is proper unto him, the *other* is but borrowed ; the *one* inwardly flows from him,

him, the *other* is inwardly fixed upon him. Almighty God 'may be said to meafure his *Judgments* by the *Ordinary Cubit*, but his *Mercies* by the *Cubit* of the *Sanctuary*, twice as big. The *Primitive Christians* lookt upon *Good Nature* to be fuch an Effential part of *Religion*, That *Tertullian* tells us, the *Professors* of *Christianity* were at firft call'd not *Christiani*, but *Chreftiani*, from a word importing *Sweetness of Temper*. And we know, it was the great Diftinguifhing Character of the *Christians* of Old, given 'em by their profeft Enemies, *Ecce ut Christiani ament* : Behold how thefe *Christians* love one another. From all this (then) we may inferr, That true *Christianity* is the *beft natur'd* Inftitution in the World ; and that fo far as any Church is departed from *Good Nature*, and becomes cruel and barbarous fo far is it degenerated from *Christianity*. But fuch has been the Misfortune of thefe latter Ages, That this bleffed Religion (fo apt

are

are the beſt Things to corrupt in
procefs of time) is ſo much miſtaken
by ſome Men, that under pretence
thereof, they act the moſt Barbarous and Inhumane Actions; and
in a moſt prepoſterous Manner think,
that the beſt way to advance *Religi-*
on, is to baniſh Peace.   But it is
wonderful to me, That, that which
was deſign'd to make us Happy in
another World, ſhou'd by its Diviſions make us moſt Miſerable in *this*;
and that which was ordain'd for the
ſaving of Mens *Souls*, ſhou'd be made
uſe of to take away their *Lives*,
or, what is more valuable, their
Liberties.

> *Of all the* Tyrannies *on Humane*
>   *Kind*
> *The Worſt is that which* Perſecutes
>   *the Mind.*
> *Let us but weigh at what Offence*
>   *we ſtrike,*
> *'Tis but becauſe we cannot* Think
>   *alike.*

In

In punishing of This *we over-*
throw
The Laws of Nations *and of* Nature *too.*

DRYD. Hind *and* Panther

And what is all this Bustle for?
Only to *force* Men to the same O-
pinion in Matters of *Religion*, a
Thing which the Experience of all
Ages hath shewn to be both Unsafe
and Impracticable. Alas! 'Tis a
fond Imagination to think, That
Religion can be impos'd on Men;
or that we can bind the *Understand-*
ings and *Wills* of Men with the
same Fetters we do their Bodies.
'Tis true, did *Religion* consist only in some *External Conformities,*
then *External Force* might bear
some Proportion to it : But *Reli-*
gion, we know, is seated in those
Faculties, to which *outward Violence*
can have no access. 'Tis *Reason*
then,

then, not *Force* muſt gain the Con-
queſt. *Force* in matters of *Opinion*
is ſo far from doing any good, that
it is often apt to do hurt ; for it is
not in any Mans power, to alter
his *Opinion* whenever he has a Mind
to't ; Indeed, it were very well if
he cou'd, for by that Means he
might cure many Inconveninences of
his Life: As for inſtance, if a Man who
lies under a ſevere fit of the *Colick*,
or the *Stone*, could but perſwade
himſelf he was at eaſe and felt
no pain ; or if a Man, who is
plunder'd or Impriſon'd, cou'd but
imagine he was kindly us'd, he
might then ſleep without any diſturbance : But, I ſay, ſince a Man cannot alter his Opinion when he liſts,
nor ever does heartily, or reſolute-
ly but when he cannot do otherwiſe,
then to uſe *Force* may make a Man
a *Hypocrite*, but never to be a *Real
Convert*. No wonder then, the
Heathens lived ſo quietly, without
any Quarrel, or War of Opinions in
Matters of *Religion :* For the
their

their feveral Cities profefs'd the Worfhip of feveral *Deitie's*,. yet we
read not of any War which fprung
from that Diverfity. The *Poets*
have made the *Gods* enter into *Factions* and Quarrels for *Common-
Wealths*, but *Common-Wealths* never.
did the fame for their *Gods*. This
Quiet and Happinefs, which to the
fhame and fcandal of the *Chriftian*
Name was enjoy'd four thoufand
Years among the *Heathen*, continued
fo long and fo uninterrupted, becaufe every Man , following the
Rules of his own judgment, allowed
that *Liberty* to others which he
found fo neceffary for himfelf. And
even the *Stoicks* themfelves, who en-
flav'd the *Will*, durft never attempt
this violence to the *Underftanding*.
But (God knows) among us *Chriftians* it has (unhappily) fallen
out quite otherwife ; for the
leaft Difference fets us together by
the Ears, and then we Stigmatize
one another with the Blackeft Characters and the moft Reproachful
Terms

Terms. When People once feparate and randezvous themfelves into di-ftinct *Sects* and *Parties*, they always confine their kindnefs to their own *Party*, and look with a Scornful and Malignant Afpect upon all the reft of Mankind ; thofe that are not with-in the Pale of their *Church*, can-not be within the Sphear of their *Charity*. For they think it no part of their Duty to Commiferate or Supply the Wants of the *Unrege-nerate*. As the *Poet* defcribes the *Jewifh Bigots*.

> *Non Monftrare vias, eadem nifi fa-*
> *cra Colenti,*
> *Quæfitum ad fontem folos deducere*
> *Verpos.*

They would not fo much as di-rect the Way to any but a *Circum-cis'd Brother*, nor beftow a Cup of Cold Water upon a Thirfty *Samari-tan*. And thus, according to *Hu-dibras*,

Do all Religions flock together,
Like Tame *and* Wild Fowl *of a*
Feather.

MoſtMen are ſo fond of their own *Opinions* in Matters of *Religion*, that whoever oppoſes them, are lookt upon not only as *their* Enemies, but as *God's* too : And therefore when Paſſion is fired with *Religious Zeal*, nothing can temper its outragious Heats; But it works the Minds of Men into rancour and bitterneſs, and drives 'em into all manner of Savage and Inhumane Practices: Nay, and which is ſtill the more deplorable, it is conſtantly obſerved, That all *Parties* are much Warmer and more Furious in defending thoſe *Points* for which there is leaſt *Reaſon*; for, ſays *Tillotſon*, what Men want of *Reaſon* for their *Opinions*, they uſually ſupply and make up in *Rage*. We are now come to that paſs, that we cannot with patience

S   tience

tience admit of *other* Mens *Opinions*, nor endure that *our own* shou'd be oppos'd. As it was in the *Lacede-monian* Army, almost all were *Captains*; so in our Disputes, all will be *Leaders* and we look on our selves to be much affronted, if others think not as we do. Men are as apt to defend their *Opinions*, as their *Property*, and wou'd take it as well to have their *Titles* to their *Estates* question'd as their *Sense*. And it often happens, that the Weaker their *Opinions* are, the fonder they are of them; just like Indulgent Mothers, that are most tender of those Children that are Weakest. Hence many Men are so possest with their own *Phancies* and *Opinions*, that they take them for *Oracles*, and think they *see Visions*, when at the same time (God knows) they do but *Dream Dreams*. In a Word, most Men are so fond of their own *Opinions* that they make themselves the *Standards* of Wisdom,

dom, to which all are Bound to conform, and whoever weighs not in their Ballance, be his Reasons never so Weighty, they write *Zekel* upon them. But after all, *Opinions* are but *Relishes* ; and Men-differ no less in them, than in their *Tasts* and *Palats* : Therefore I may with as much reason be angry with a Man, for not being of my *Diet*, as for not being of my *Opinion*. That all Men shou'd be of the same *Opinion*, and agree in the same Conception and Apprehensions of things, is impossible, and no more to be expected in this Life, than that all Mens Faces and Complexions shou'd be alike, for as long as Men have different Educations, Tempers, Constitutions of Body, Inclinations of Mind , and Several Interests to serve ; so long there will be Disputes and Controversies even about matters of *Religion :* What Devilish Pride (then) is it, to endeavour (like the *Old Tyrant*) to Stretch, or

S 2   Cramp

Cramp up, every Man to the proportion of my Bed? It is certainly
the greateſt Oppreſſion and Uſurpa-
tion imaginable, to aſſault, or try
to overcome the Reaſon of another
by any thing elſe but Reaſon.   The
way to our future happineſs has been
perpetually diſputed throughout the
World, and muſt be left at laſt to
the *Impreſſions* made upon every
Mans *Belief* or *Conſcience*, either by
Naturel or Supernatural Arguments
and Means ; which *Impreſſions* Men
may diſguiſe or diſſemble, but noMan
can reſiſt.   For *Belief* is no more
in a Man's Power, than his Stature,
or his Feature: And he that tells
me, I muſt change my *Opinion* for
his, becauſe it is the truer and better, without other Arguments, that
have to me the force of Conviction,
may as well tell me, I muſt change
my *Gray Eyes* for others like his that
are *Black*; becauſe theſe are lovelier,
or more in eſteem. He that tells me,
I muſt *Inform* my ſelf ; has reaſon,

if

if I do it not: But if I endeavour
it all that I can, and perhaps more
than he ever did, and yet still differ
from him; And he, that it may be
is idle, will have me Study on, and
Inform my self better, and so to the
end of my Life; Then I easily un-
derstand what he means by *Informing*,
which is in short,that I must do it till
I come to be of his *Opinion*.If he that
perhaps pursues his Pleasures or Interests as much or more than I do;
And allows me to have as good sense
as he has in all other matters; tells
me, I should be of his *Opinion*, but
that *Passion* or *Interest* blinds me;
unless he can convince me *How* or
Where this lies, he is but where he
was, only 'pretends to know me
better than I do my self, who cannot
imagine, why I should not have as
much care of *my*Soul as he has of *his*.
A Man that tells me, my *Opinions*
are absurd or ridiculous, impertinent
or unreasonable, because they differ
from *his*, seems to intend a *Quarrel*

inſtead of a *Diſpute* ; and calls me
Fool or *Madman* with a little more
Circumſtance ; Tho perhaps I paſs
for one as well in my Senſes as *He*,
as pertinent in Talk, and as prudent
in Life : yet theſe are the common
Civilities in Religious Arguments of
Conceited Men, who talk much of
Right Reaſon, but mean always *their
own* ; and make their private Imagination the meaſure of general truth.
But ſuch Language determins all between us, and the Diſpute comes to
end in three Words at laſt, which
it might as well have ended in at
firſt, that *he is in the Right, and I am
in the Wrong.* At this rate, and in this
obſtinate manner, do the generality
of Men act in the Concerns of *Religion,* as thinking they cannot ſhew
too much Heat and Zeal upon that
Subject. When once Mens Minds have
taken up Schemes and *Ideas* of *Religion*
right or wrong they are reſolv'd to
defend them, and every thing within their reach is preſt and made to
ſerve

ferve in defence of thofe preconceiv'd
Opinions. Even *Scripture* it felf,
but the genuine Senfe be what it will,
is too often made ufe of to thefe
purpofes; Nay, if there be any one
Word, or Phrafe in the *Bible*, that
Sounds like the *Tinkling* of fuch
Mens Fancies, prefently they conclude, that God himfelf fpeaks their
Language. And thus do they ftamp
Divinity on their wildeft and moft
extravagant *Opinions*, twifting and
twining the *Scripture* as they have
a mind to't : They faften their own
Conceits upon God ; and like the
Harlot in the Book of *Kings* do
they take their dead and putrified
Fancies, and lay them in the Bo-
fome of *Scripture*. But thefe Men
deal with *Scripture* juft as *Chymifts*
do with Natural Bodies, tortur-
ing them to extract that out of
them, which God and Nature never put in them. And therefore
no wonder, 'we find fuch Diverfity
of *Opinions* in matters of *Religion*,

for if we ſtrive to *give* unto *Scri-pture*, and not to *receive* from it the Senſe, we may eaſily deduce what Inference we pleaſe and likewiſe eſtabliſh whatever Notions we think fit. *Religious Diſputes* are of a *Prolifick* Nature, eſpecially when they are manag'd by Men of Art and Sophiſtry, as may appear by the Elaborate Trifles of the *Schoolmen.* Indeed when I conſider the Subtile Diviſions and Nice Diſtinctions of theſe Men, I cannot but fancy, they had the power of Working Miracles; Queſtions in their Hands, Multiplying in the Breaking, like the *Loaves* in our *Saviour's* ; Tho' I muſt confeſs to very different purpoſes, no ſolid Nouriſhment being deriv'd from the *One*, but on the Contrary *Stones* given us inſtead of *Bread*, and thoſe too, even to fling at one another. Little advantage (then) has our *Religion* receiv'd from theſe Men, the beſt of whoſe Curioſities, and Learned

Trifles

Trifles, are but like *Paint* on *Glaß*, which ferves only to hinder and intercept the Light. But as our Differences in *Religion* are many, fo, that which aggravates ourMisfortune is,that thefeDifferences have (many of them)been grounded upon the flighteft, and moft minute matters,and have often times proceeded from the moft Inconfiderable Beginings.What was*Religion* the better for that long difpute concerning the day on which *Eafter* was to be obfery'd ? Or did it fignifie any thing to *Religion*, what *Cecilian* or his *Ordainers* were efpecially, in the Age after they were dead ? And yet not only a Seperation and violent Rage, but a great Effufion of Blood, with the other difmal Confequences of that blind Fury, follow'd upon this, and the *Africans* continued Quarrelling about it, till the *Vandals* came, and deftroy'd both the one and the other. But I need not go fo

far

far from home for Inſtances of this Kind ; ſince our own Hiſtories do furniſh us with Examples of this Nature. One could not reaſonably have imagin'd, that the Diſpute concerning *Hoods* and *Surplices* could have riſe to ſo great a Height. Who could e-ver have thought, that an old Womans Muttering againſt the *Liturgy,* when it was firſt introduced into *Scotland,* ſhould have prov'd the firſt beginning of the late Civil Wars ? And yet in Fact that it was ſo, every Body knows. Thus we ſee, that one Conteſt Breeds another, and that which perhaps began at a *Speculative* Point, ends in a *Practical* one; and that which begins in ſome *Rite* or *Ceremony,* grows at laſt to a Breach in Matters of *Faith.* And thus it is beyond all Diſpute, that many of the Conteſts about *Myſteries* Began at

ſome

fome unwary Expreffions, in which the *one fide* faften'd ill Senfes on the Words fpoken by the *other* ; and the *other*, rather than yield fo far, for Peace fake, as to explain themfelves, chofe rather to juftifie their Words in any Sence, than to retract or mollifie them.

I have often-times been amaz'd to fee, with how much Zeal and Fury fome Men have defended the ufe of *Ceremonies*, as if they were really effential to *Religion* ; whereas nothing has been a greater Clog or Impediment to *Religion*, than the mixing it with too many *Ceremonies*. We know it hath been the conftant obfervation, that the Life and Vigour of *Chriftianity* never decay'd more, than when *Ceremonies* multiplied moft. *Chriftian Religion* is a Plain, Simple, Eafie thing ; *Chrift* commends his Yoke to us by the
eafinefs

eafinefs of it, and his Burthen by the lightnefs of it. It was an excellent Teftimony which *Ammianus Marcellinus*, a Heathen, gave to *Chriftianity*, when fpeaken of *Conftantius*, that *he had Spoil'd the Beauty of Chriftianity, by Muffling it up in Superftitious Obfervations*. And it is as true which *Erafmus* faid in Anfwer to the *Sorbonifts*, that *External Ceremonies teach us Backwards, and bring us back from Chrift to Mofes*. It is not to be imagin'd by any Sober Man, that the Lord of Heaven and Earth, who is fo Jealous of his own Worfhip, that under the *Law* he feverly prohibited the *Adding to*, or *Diminifhing* one Tittle from what he had commanded, and under the *Gofpel* gave no other Commiffion, than to teach according to what he had commanded; 'tis not I fay to be imagin'd, that he hath left his Worfhip to the Invention of corrupt,

frail

frail Man, inclinable above all things to Superſtition and Idolatry, and who are by Nature endleſly various in their Sence, Imaginations and Underſtandings: This certainly ſeems highly irrational, and to accuſe *Chriſt* of not having been as a *Son*, ſo careful of his Church, as *Moſes* a *Servant* was of the Church of God under the *Law* : For had *Chriſt* intended to have left his Church under a *Negative* Obedience in Worſhip, making all things Lawful that he had not forbidden, the Command had been as readily made, to do whatſoever he had not prohibited, as it was to do whatſoever he hath commanded. The Learned and Ingenious Mr. *Hales* tells us, That to charge *Churches* and *Liturgies* with things unneceſſary, was the firſt Beginning of all Superſtition. And agreeably hereunto , does Biſhop *Bramhal,* in his Diſcourſe of *Schiſm,* profeſs to all the World, That the transforming of *Indifferent Opinions*

into

into *Neceſſary Articles* of *Faith*, hath been that *Inſana.Laurus*, or *Curſed Bay-Tree*, ·the Cauſe of all our Differences and Contentions. The *Ancient Fathers* call'd the *Creed Symbolum*, the *Shot*, and *Total Summ* of *Faith*; but ſince their Times we have had a great many *after-Reckonings* brought us in ; to which it we will not pay our Belief, our Souls muſt be arreſted without *Bail* upon pain of Eternal Damnation.　In the Beginning of the *Reformation*, C E-R E M O N I E S were retain'd to win upon the People, who were then generally *Papiſts,* and doated upon old uſages, and not as the neceſſary conditions of Communion ; they were retain'd not to ſhut out of doors the *Proteſtants*, as in the late Reigns they were us'd, but to invite in the *Romaniſts*, which was their original End ; But there's nothing more common, than for *Inſtitutions* to degenerate, and be perverted from the firſt Reaſons of
　　　　　　　　　　their

their usage, and yet still to plead the Credit of their *Originals* : Thus *Indulgences*, and *Remission* of *Sins*, were first granted to all that wou'd engage in the *Holy War*, to reco-ver the *Sepulchre* of *Christ* out of the Hands of the *Saracens* ; but in process of time they were dispenced to them who would Massacre the *Waldenses* and *Albigenses*, and such as cou'd not Obey the **Tyranny** of the *Romish* Faction : Thus was the *Inquisition* first set up **to discover the** Hypocritical *Moors* in *Spain* ; but the Edge of it since turn'd against the **Protestants**. And thus were the *Ce-remonies* perverted, at first made a *Key* to let in the *Papists*, and since made a *Lock* to shut out *Protestants*.

F I N I S.

www.ingramcontent.com/pod-product-compliance
Lightning Source LLC
Chambersburg PA
CBHW031333070726
47496CB00018B/1848